LIFE
ON THE
ASH
HEAP

LIFE
ON THE
ASH
HEAP

JOB FIGHTS GOD'S
BATTLE FOR HIM

JIM McGUIGGAN

www.covenantpublishing.com

P.O. Box 390 Webb City, Missouri 64870
Call toll free at 877.673.1015

Library of Congress Cataloging-in-Publication Data
McGuiggan, Jim, 1937–
  Life on the ash heap : Job fights God's battle for him / Jim McGuiggan
    p. cm.
Includes bibliographical references.
  ISBN 1-892435-22-5 (pbk.)
  1. Bible. O.T. Job—Meditations. I. Title.
  BS1415.54.M34 2003
  223'.106—dc21
                        2003005947

DEDICATION

For Anne

TABLE OF CONTENTS

I
INTRODUCTORY MATTERS

INTRODUCTION

God knows who wrote the book of Job but nobody else does. Although we can't be sure when the book was written, the central human character is Job who lived in the days of the patriarchs. The pivotal events are these: Satan slanders this righteous, prosperous man and God goes to his defense in a very remarkable way. The rest of the book takes its departure from what the first two chapters tell us.

Here's the Story Line

Job, a man of outstanding piety and righteousness is also a very wealthy man. God praises him in the presence of Satan who insists that Job has no integrity, no genuine love for God but instead sees God as a meal ticket. If God withdrew the blessings, Satan said, Job would forsake him because Job cared nothing about righteousness or true piety. The material blessings are withdrawn but Job remains loyal. Satan insists that Job would forsake God if his life were threatened but illness and disfigurement fail to turn Job from God (1–2).

When his friends arrive, the agony-filled Job expresses his deep grief and wishes he were dead. That begins a series of exchanges between Job and his friends that becomes bitter. The friends who share the same basic message and approach assure him that if he will only repent of his sin against God, God will receive him back into favor and restore the blessings he has lost. Job refuses to admit he has done anything wrong and the tension deepens as they go on. Frustrated with the speeches of the friends, Job speaks directly and formally to God and calls for a meeting (3–31).

Then a younger observer (Elihu) speaks up. He offers himself as a sort of referee between Job and his friends, not only because he's dissatisfied with the speeches of both Job and his friends, but because Job has been begging for such a character. Elihu makes his own contribution to the discussion (32–37).

It's at this point God answers Job's persistent call for a response from him. Out of a storm he speaks and convicts Job of his ignorance and his powerlessness. Job admits his ignorance and repents of his pride-filled words and self-righteousness (38–42:6).

As a conclusion to it all God favorably compares what Job said with what his friends had to say and makes Job the mediator and priest for them. He then restores Job to an even greater state of blessedness than he had before (42:7-17).

So the usual very basic outline, while it hides difficulties, gives us a summary of the book's structure.

I. The Opening Scenes (1:1–2:13)
II. The Exchanges between Job and His Friends (3–31)
III. The Speech of Elihu (32–37)
IV. God's Address to Job (38–41)
V. Job's Brief Response to God (42:1-6)
VI. The Conclusion of the Drama (42:7-16)

Why Was the Book Written?

James Crenshaw thinks it's difficult if not impossible to know why the book was written. Matatiahu Tsevat feels sure it was written to turn the rest of the Bible on its ear. It was written he thinks to show that no moral government operates in this life or in this world. William P. Brown is sure it was written to give a new answer to a question like, "What is a good person?" or "What is good character?" Georg Fohrer and Philip Yancey think it was written to show us how people should live under suffering. Gregory Parsons who follows Samuel Terrien thinks it's written to show that humanity is utterly dependent on God's sovereign grace and is called to respond to God in faith. Sylvia Huberman Scholnick thinks the book is to show that God is King as well as Judge so that the notion of "justice" would be expanded. Numerous authors think it was written to explain the existence of suffering in the world and in particular why bad things happen to good people.

Major Messages of the Book

Despite the difficulties ranged against finding one central purpose for the book many see what they believe to be major purposes and messages in it.

The book stresses the limits of human wisdom. The reader is given the full explanation for Job's terrible ordeal and is then made to watch while five (including Elihu) wise, experienced and God-fearing men run around in circles, repeating themselves, in the vain attempt to proclaim or uncover the truth. In light of the book of Job we're to admit that an event may be "blessing" even if it looks like stark "curse."

Whatever else the book of Job parades before us, it is a piece of wisdom that teaches us that the wise should recognize the limits of human wisdom even when that wisdom comes from God. It illustrates well Proverbs 20:24, one of the "limiting" proverbs which offers, "A man's steps are directed by the LORD. How then can anyone understand his own way?" Or 16:9, "In his heart a man plans his course, but the LORD determines his steps." The outcome of this is that we should be modest and do our level best to stay off God's throne because only *he* is big enough to fill it.

The book calls humans to embrace the mysteries in life in a spirit of trust. Incredible as it may seem to us at times, God put a bewildered Job to grief and still expected him to maintain his trust in the God who had been his lifelong friend. Job's initial trust and his later confession and repentance are the right responses to mystery in a world governed by a loving and righteous Lord. Job isn't told what happened over his head (so to speak) but then the book wasn't written for Job—it was written for us. Job isn't intended to be an example we're to follow in everything but he certainly is intended to be an inspiration to us as one struggling through the darkness toward the light.

The book insists that the loving devotion of humans toward God has cosmic consequences. We must allow the exchanges between God and Satan to affect our understanding of the point of the book. Although Job didn't know it, he was fighting God's fight for him against the evil forces of cynicism and darkness in the universe. Job's quarrel with God was a lover's quarrel and we're to remember that God is counting on Job to live gallantly as well as passionately.

The book insists that the blessings of life are always the gracious provision of God. The Job who was restored to material and social prosperity had been scandalously unfair to God in his self-centeredness, so we know he hadn't earned the return to blessing. Numerous texts in the book tell us that even the wicked receive their blessings from God. In God's speech to Job we're told that the animals are provided for even though they are oblivious to God's hand in it.

The book insists that God is sovereign and will go his own way to accomplish his loving and holy purposes without asking man's permission. When God finally spoke to Job, he spoke to him out of a storm and it wasn't an explanation he offered. While God came in the whirlwind to do Job good, he apologized for nothing! This is not to say that God has the right to pervert justice but he does have the right as sovereign to make radical demands of us if it serves his holy and loving purposes for mankind.

The book insists that a life of trust and loyalty can exist even when the truster is far from calm and far from quietly submissive. I say enough later about the wrongs of snarling mean accusations against God but the book does present God's hero as just that, *God's* man, whose integrity is expressed in weeping and anger, in earnest pleading and hot protest, in gentle prayers and scathing denunciations. This trusting hero was a civil war, a mob. He wasn't what thoughtless people often insist is the picture of the model servant. He wasn't the neat, controlled, even-tempered, calmly-assured, smiling-through-it-all figure who knows "God is in charge."

One of the purposes of the book of Job may well be to set before us the ugly picture of self-righteousness in full pursuit of the lame and ragged as they try to shake us off. Once the debate got going it's clear that while the friends were happy to sit on God's throne for him they weren't especially interested to enter into Job's heart and life and pain.

When Reading the Book
Remember: The repetition is deliberate.

The repetitive nature of the book serves an important purpose. For many of us the book of Job is like a train ride that begins well, with interesting things to see, but very quickly leaves the interesting behind, runs for most of the trip through mainly unchanging and dull stretches, and then picks up just before we arrive at the station.

A similar thing happens at the beginning of the Bible. A blaze of creative activity is followed by drama well told which takes us through, say, Exodus 18, the rhythm falters a bit until the drama resumes in chapters 32–34 then arrhythmia sets in again and becomes almost unbearable when we arrive at Leviticus and large chunks of Numbers.

Let's face it, a lot of the rules and regulations, lists, genealogies and descriptions in the nineteen chapters in Exodus, the twenty-seven in Leviticus and the large number in Numbers were redundant before many years passed. How could they be of interest? And if they aren't of real interest there's no motivation for plowing through them—so we skip them!

But they're of vital and abiding interest for numerous reasons. Let me mention this one (because it makes contact with Job) and leave you to work on others. *The Old Testament is strong on repetition as a method of teaching.*

The countless details about the Tabernacle are given not only for information purposes; they're given to stress *the centrality and importance of worship!* Gabriel Josipovichi points out the difference between the making of the Tabernacle and of the Golden Calf.

In Exodus the making of the Golden Calf is described in *three verses* (32:2-4) while the making of the Tabernacle is described in *thirteen chapters.* In the making of the Calf you have the impression of impulsiveness, speed and passion which wants what it wants then and there. It's all done in the twinkling of an eye, the materials are thrown in the fire and out jumps this calf (32:21-24).

In the case of the Tabernacle there is a "loving lingering" over the details by people whose hearts were moved by the Spirit of God. You need to imagine the joyful groups of women and men working together day after day on tiny details, carefully fitting things together, producing harmony and richness as the Tent rose out of the dust in the desert, a place for God to live in at the heart of the nation.

The repetition in the book of Job serves a purpose. Among other things we are being told *these men have nothing further to say!* Their wisdom has reached its end. All their wise thoughts have been exhausted and they are no nearer the truth about Job's condition than they were when they started.

The reader is *supposed* to sense the repetitiveness, he is *supposed* to experience the feeling that comes when one hears the same thing over and over again and it's no more to the point than it was the first time. Allow yourself to feel the slight boredom and the frustration (which must have galled all the disputants) and *feel* the message that human wisdom has its limits.

The reader is *supposed* to agree with Job who quickly recognizes that only God can deal with this situation (13:2-3 illustrates this). He knows *he* doesn't have the answer and that his wise friends are just as ignorant.

Remember: No one in the book believed in rigid retribution.

Numerous scholars insist that Job and his friends believed in rigid retribution. That is, they say their moral world was like a Coke machine, so much righteousness in and so much blessing out; so much evil in and measured punishment out. A pound of blessing or cursing for a pound of goodness or evil. These scholars use phrases like *quid pro quo* retribution or a *mechanically exact* arrangement or they speak of it being "rigidly exact." This is manifestly untrue!

It's true they all believed in divine retribution (as do the rest of the Bible characters, including Jesus and Paul), but they did *not* believe it was all mechanical nor precisely worked out. We know this because they all speak of innocent people suffering and wicked people prospering. Job's friends will finally accuse him of having been wicked all his life, which makes it clear they didn't think in terms of rigid repayment for sins. Job argues that there are innocents all over the place who are being oppressed.

But he didn't change his view on divine retribution. His last speech tells us he still believed in it. The truth is, he *never* believed in a rigid doctrine of retribution. That's not where Job's problem lay!

Remember: Don't expect calm reasoning in the book.

Job is in awful pain once the troubles come so we mustn't treat what he says as if it were calmly delivered theology. His agonized cries aren't statements of doctrinal positions held they are cries of hurt amazement . . . as if he were going around telling everyone who would listen, "Can you believe God would do such a thing? Isn't that disgraceful?" He admits his pain has made his speech reckless (6:3) and he does what we all do when we're in agony— he contradicts himself.

On the one hand he wishes he were dead and on the other he laments the fact that his life is passing too quickly. One moment he's saying God doesn't bother to punish the wicked and the next he says God will punish his friends if they continue to tell lies in God's defense. At one point he hates God and wishes he could die so he wouldn't have to deal with him ever again and later he confesses he misses God terribly and wishes things were as they once were.

Remember: There was always more than one option.

The friends did not *have to* believe Job was very wicked. They *could have* believed him when he said he was completely innocent. They had known his life's history, had heard no breath of scandal or had any reason to accuse him of wickedness. It's true they believed in retribution but they had seen the innocent suffer (orphans and widows, for example) so they didn't *need* to take the cynical view of him that they finally took!

And Job did not *have to* take the view of God his friends dished out. He had the same traditions and experience his friends had. He himself (see chapters 29 and 31) eased the suffering of the innocent so he knew that calamity can come on the guiltless. He didn't *need* to think what had happened to him proved God to be treacherous and unfaithful or that he was holding Job guilty of some crime.

Tsevat tells us that the book of Job is saturated in traditional Jewish theology. That makes sense to me. This can only underscore the truth that all of the figures in the book would have been well acquainted with "innocent suffering." Why do we have to read it as though they had never heard of such a thing? You might think they never recognized such a reality but they speak of it again and again.

Remember: Being a sufferer doesn't make us infallible.

This is a hard saying but it's demonstrated throughout the book of Job. When we're the ones enduring terrible loss we're tempted to think that we're in some privileged position to know the mind and purpose of God. We hear so much nonsense talked about our situation, don't you see, that we could be forgiven if we think no one knows anything. People offer this piece of advice or this insight or that theological explanation and we, sensing that so much of it is wholly irrelevant to our case and needs, endure their ignorance as long as we can. We're often too polite to tell them they're talking drivel. It isn't only the ignorance we hear pouring out of others that moves us toward "expert" status, it's how people invite us to speak the complete word on the tough questions of life and it isn't always easy to say we're just as bewildered as the next person. (Of course there are things the sufferer can learn that others can't. The wisest and most sympathetic reader of the book of Job can never gain what Job gained. But that's not what I'm speaking about here.) People can learn from suffering but they rarely become "experts." That requires an additional something else.

Remember: Even truth must be handled truthfully.

To judge the character and truth of what Job's friends said we have to note not only *what* they said, but also what they meant to do with what they said. For example, Elihu insists that God is infinitely greater than humans—that is true. But he used that truth against Job to show him that God didn't care whether humans were good or bad—and that's a lie (see 35:5-7 and 22:2-3)! Sometimes you can speak truth in support of a lie. At one point Job called his friends false witnesses on God's behalf.

The friends finally came to believe that Job was a hypocritical sinner and that God was punishing him for it—which was untrue! But they spoke truths about God's wisdom, power and justice in support of what was untrue. So when we take their speeches as a whole we are to judge them by where they were going with them. This helps to make sense of 42:7 where God rebukes them for not speaking the truth about him "as my servant Job has." God was not denying that the friends spoke many truths, it's what they were doing with the truths that made them false witnesses. What is true of the friends is also true of Job. Job's bottom line was true although he blundered on the way there. The bottom line for the friends was untrue although they spoke truths on the way to it.

Remember: The god Job was mad at didn't exist.

The god Job attacked was a fiction, a distorted image, someone that didn't exist. It was the kind of god the true God would attack! The god Job was attacking was heartless and a betrayer of friendship but it was a god he imagined, it was the creation of his agony, the goading of his friends and a misguided interpretation of the facts.

In raving against a god like that, Job was actually calling for a God with integrity. Without knowing he was doing it he was proving he wasn't the "yes man" Satan said he was. Again this helps us to explain 42:7 where God said Job (who had done all this yelling about "God") had spoken right things about him. The accusations were against the god Job thought had taken God's place (so to speak); they were against the god Job thought God had become. He was calling God back to his "old self," which was a God of righteousness and faithfulness.

Now it isn't all good news because the God who put Job to grief was the true God and Job was attacking the one who was hurting him. As the text gives it, when Job blames *God* for his trouble, he's laying the blame at the right doorstep (see 1:16; 42:11) but he had the wrong explanation. The God who worked in and through Job wouldn't be domesticated nor would he be imprisoned by general truths of wisdom. If Job's *interpretation* of the situation had been true, then God would have been treacherous and heartless. *That* God would not be fit to be worshiped. *That* God would need to be convicted, would need to be held to account, would need to be denounced. And that's precisely what Job engaged in.

But even while he rages some of what Job says shows he isn't completely satisfied with his own interpretation of things. He appeals to God for mercy, which says he isn't convinced that God is heartless. He wonders if maybe God won't hide him in Sheol for a while and then bring him out and vindicate him. At one point he warns his friends against defending God with lies because God doesn't approve of lies and will punish them for it. In the book of Job there's more than one "Job" and more than one "God."

Remember: What the book is built on.

Satan/God exchanges in 1:6-12 and 2:1-6 are the pivot points for the rest of the book. So wherever we wander, we must take those exchanges seriously as we look for the central thrust(s) of the book of Job. Furthermore, when people say God was "testing" Job, and there is some truth in that because it did test Job, still, that's not the best way to state what happened in the prologue. One great writer said the narrative opens with "God afflicting Job in order to discover whether Job's piety depends only upon his prosperity." That isn't correct. God didn't subject Job to this grief to find out *if* Job was truly righteous; he did it to demonstrate what he already knew, that Job was indeed righteous. The trials were not to discover if righteousness existed but to uncover an even deeper righteousness that God already knew was there.

Again, while there may be some truth in saying that Satan was slyly impugning God's character, it's a mistake to make too much of that since it isn't clearly in the text. It's Job's character that is under attack by Satan. It is *Job* not Satan who attacks God's integrity and he does it in the dialogues. But even there Job's attack on God's integrity is an extended demonstration of his own integrity, which is what the prologue is all about.

Remember: It was not Satan who took Job's blessings away.

It is clear just from the reading that Satan was given power to afflict Job. It's equally clear from the text that Satan thinks he is only doing the bidding of God. Satan twice says to God "stretch out your hand and strike" (1:11; 2:5) and God chooses to do that. In the narrative Satan is simply God's agent or instrument—God does it through Satan.

It is important to the reading of the entire book and its message that we accept the truth that it is *God* who withdraws his blessings. *Without exception* every character in the book lays the calamity at God's feet. Job does it repeatedly, the friends argue it all the way through, Elihu insists on it, Satan challenges God to do it and the narrator expressly lays Job's troubles at the Lord's feet (42:11). Does it make any difference if we drive a nail into a wall using a hammer or a rock? That God used Satan to carry out his will in Job's affairs is his choosing between a hammer and a rock. To say, "It was Satan who robbed Job of his blessings" empties the book of its tension and point.

Remember: What Job's central problem was.

Job had seen God as his lordly Friend (29:1-5), the Sovereign of all that is. A Friend to whom Job had been faithful. Under the devastating calamities and with a bit of help from his earthly friends Job drew the conclusion that God had proved faithless, had turned against one of his loyal servants. Knowing that he had not turned from God, in his anger, pain and frustration he was willing to accuse the silent Lord of treachery and proclaim himself more righteous than his Lord.

This feeling of lost friendship, the sense of having been abandoned, almost unhinged him. It entirely misses the point of the book to begin with questions about competing systems of retribution. Job who knows he's innocent is asking, "Has God been righteous (faithful) to his commitment to humanity and to me in particular?" And we who have been expressly told what the situation is are asked to watch how the "play" develops. The book isn't written to *argue* Job's innocence. It isn't written to show God is punishing an innocent man. It isn't written to examine seriously the pros and cons of competing retributive systems. It isn't written for the benefit of the specific characters in the drama—it's written for us.

Remember: The book is written for you.

Reading some scholars is like licking carpet—not a pleasant experience, and often it's no more nutritious than licking carpet. Still, it's hard to overestimate the richness, the depth and insight that many of these men and women uncover for us. But each of us must read for herself/himself. Within the parameters of a sensible reading of the book we are to eat and drink and be nourished in a faith in God that's fit for grown-ups.

Some people have suggested that Job was a hard sort of a man who was more concerned about outward religious observances than the real issues of life. Amazing view that is. If we want to know what he's like we have to read his "defense" (see chapters 29–31). In that section, the scholars tell us, he challenges God to meet him in court and disprove the claim of innocence he's now making. There's no reason to believe that what he says about himself is untrue, because whatever else he believes, he believes God hears him and if he is lying God will point it out. What follows connects with 29–31 so read the chapters for yourself and note the richness and generosity of his life.

II
LIFE IN THE SUNSHINE

Reading some scholars is like licking carpet—
not a pleasant experience, and often it's no more
nutritious than licking carpet. Still, it's hard to
overestimate the richness, the depth and insight
that many of these men and women uncover for us.
But each of us must read for herself/himself.
Within the parameters of a sensible reading of
the book we are to eat and drink and be nourished
in a faith in God that's fit for grown-ups.

I

MAKING HEARTS SING

"...remembering the words the Lord Jesus himself
said:'It is more blessed to give than to receive.'"

Acts 20:35

"Whoever heard me spoke well of me, and those who saw me
commended me, because I rescued the poor who cried for help,
and the fatherless who had none to assist him. The man who was
dying blessed me; I made the widow's heart sing" (29:11-13).
That's what Job says about himself but he isn't bragging. He may
well have been a bit red-faced and felt like Paul in 2 Corinthians
11:17 and 21, and elsewhere who said he was forced to do what
made him feel like a fool. No, Job isn't boasting, he's desperate. In
his desperation he told of his generous heart and liberal way.

Elsewhere I've echoed the experience of novelist and social
critic George Gissing who went to the aid of a little boy he found
crying. Only recently did I come across the story told by the writer
himself and only then did I understand its deeper significance. It
was in the year he died (1903) that he wrote *The Private Papers of
Henry Ryecroft*, a novel (of sorts) based on his own life. Here in the
great man's own words is what happened.

Near a hamlet, in a lonely spot by a woodside, I came
upon a little lad of perhaps ten years old, who, his head
hidden in his arms against a tree trunk, was crying bitterly. I asked him what was the matter, and after a little trouble—he was better than a mere bumpkin—I learned that,
having been sent with sixpence to pay a debt, he had lost
the money. The poor little fellow was in a state of mind
which in a grave man would be called the anguish of
despair; he must have been crying for a long time; every

muscle in his face quivered as if under torture, his limbs shook; his eyes, his voice, uttered such misery as only the vilest criminal should be made to suffer. And it was because he had lost sixpence!

I could have shed tears with him—tears of pity and of rage at all this spectacle implied. On a day of indescribable glory, when earth and heaven shed benedictions upon the soul of man, a child, whose nature would have bidden him rejoice as only childhood may, wept his heart out because his hand had dropped a sixpenny piece! The loss was a very serious one, and he knew it; he was less afraid to face his parents, than be overcome by misery at the thought of the harm he had done them. Sixpence dropped by the wayside, and a whole family made wretched! What are the due descriptive terms for a state of "civilization" in which such a thing as this is possible? I put my hand into my pocket, and wrought sixpenny-worth of miracle.[1]

If we've never done something like that, we've always wanted to, haven't we? The delicious thrill of transforming a scene of anguish into one of disbelieving joy by writing a check is hard to equal. It makes your heart sing! There's too much needless sorrow in the world and a lot of it could be removed by a generous and wise sharing of our wealth. I know there are many problems that are only made worse by "throwing money at them" but in my own tiny little life, down the years, I've known many hundreds of situations where the generous giving of money would have changed the world for poor souls whose dreary existence was strangling them.

When you did it, don't you remember the wide eyes and the utter speechlessness? It was more than the money—the world became a different place, if only for a while. Unrelieved darkness was filled with light; despair was replaced with the possibilities and hope. Maybe things *wouldn't* always be as bad as they had been. At least once, these beaten people felt they mattered to someone. A job, a coat, a box of groceries, a debt paid, a friendship offered and hearts begin to sing.

There is money involved in this loveliness but it's more than the money, isn't it? Russian born novelist Ivan Turgenev tells how one day he met a beggar who asked for some money. "I felt all my pockets," said the writer, "no purse, watch, or handkerchief did I find. I had left them all at home. The beggar waited, and his out-stretched hand twitched and trembled slightly. Embarrassed and confused I seized the dirty hand and pressed it. 'Don't be vexed with me, brother, I have nothing with me, brother.' The beggar raised his blood-shot eyes to mine, his blue lips smiled, and he returned the pressure of the chilled fingers. 'Never mind, brother,' he stammered, 'thank you for this. This too was a gift, brother.'" Turgenev concludes, "I felt that I too had received a gift from my brother." Yes! It's *more* than the money.

And God looked down at the land of Uz and saw the needs of countless people so he blessed the family of a man called Job with *incredible* wealth. God made the man's fields simply burst with rich, abundant harvests; made his flocks and herds increase until the herdsmen and shepherds scratched their heads, not knowing where to put so many thriving animals; made his investments generate money beyond the capacity of all his banks and made his commercial trading so successful he became known as the greatest figure in the entire East.

And he knew very well where all his blessings came from. "The LORD gives," he insisted. But he knew more than that—he knew the Lord! Now *that* was life in the sunshine! Rolling in money but rich toward God this man exulted in the privilege of giving money away. Listen to the pleasure in his voice as he says:

"I made the widow's heart sing" (29:13).

Don't you love that? Let your imagination get to work on it a while. You've seen things like that happen, haven't you? And if you know God you've had the delicious pleasure of triggering such singing. The widow is heartbroken and can't stop her tears. A thousand and one things need done and she isn't able to do them. She can't make ends meet, her loneliness drains her strength, her pain makes her wonder where God is and if he knows or cares about her.

Then down the street comes a smiling Job with a well-loaded cart. What did he say to her? What was his tone? Did he hold her close without a word, respecting her suppressed sobs and blessing her with silence? And when she finally poured out her poor heart did he listen and nod, saying in that compassionate way that love-ly people have, "I know, I know"?

And as he was leaving, how much money did he press into her hand and how high did the servants pile her shelves as Job watched approvingly? Quietly and very discreetly telling the servant now and then, "Yes, and give her some more of those. Yes, and those too." What awful financial burden did he commit to take care of right away for her? And as she stared in joyful disbelief at the change in her fortunes did he whisper to her that she knew where he lived, that she was to come at any time she was in need and ask for him personally? Is that what he said? God knows! But when he left her, her heart sang!

And did his heart sing? Wouldn't yours? Knowing you've been the outstretched hand of God that banishes misery and brings joy, that obliterates gloom and brings glory! *This is life in the sunlight!*

To be unashamedly rich and to love God because it's his pleasure to let you ease burdens and mend broken hearts so that they sing. Do we have any reason to believe that Job was a prisoner of conscience because he was rich and others were poor? None at all. He probably didn't have the time; he was too busy joyfully changing the world while his Lord looked on, with admiration in his eyes. Job didn't lie at night fighting nightmares—he lay thinking of better ways to help more needy people. An interest-free loan here, a cart full of good things there, a piece of land redeemed yesterday or a free night's lodging tonight.

A bushel's worth of miracle! Singing hearts all over creation.

To have peace of mind in this area, to take pleasure in your wealth and talent; to have the heart and the compassion to be pleased to transform misery and make hearts sing—*this is life in the sunlight!* More wonderful than all this, more wonderful than how he felt about God was the way God felt about him. "There's nobody like him," said the truthful Lord of the universe. "Have you ever taken a really good look at him?" And if the cynical Satan had had the heart to see it, he would have seen one of the great glories of God's universe—a beautiful human being, brimful of life from God and spilling it everywhere he went.

2

THEY SCARCELY BELIEVED IT

"When I smiled at them, they scarcely believed it;
the light of my face was precious to them."

Job 29:24

Money is so commonly gained by immoral means that Christ once spoke of it as if it were all tainted (see Luke 16:9). And such is the corrupting power of wealth that he said rich people wouldn't make it into the kingdom (see Matthew 19:24). Though he believed neither of these extremes, he was willing to risk being misunderstood if he could get across the danger there is in our handling money.

You understand it isn't money itself that is dangerous, it's just that we're so sinfully vulnerable that when we have power (of which money is the symbol) we are deceived and become corrupted. Having a lot of power (money) deceives many of us into thinking we're a cut above the rest of humanity. Even when we acknowledge that the money is from God, we still feel superior. We must feel superior, don't you see, because God gave us this power, rather than giving it to someone else. That must say something about our qualities and wisdom. And so we demand respect. Respect that shows itself as marked, so the usual smiles and courteous treatment isn't sufficient. We aren't like the common herd so we must not be treated in the ordinary way. If there's to be no groveling, there must at least be additional fuss or an over-the-top introduction, a more solicitous attitude, a more intense look of interest when we are delivering our opinions.

None of these undesirable reactions to wealth is seen in the man from Uz. We have not even the slightest indication that he struggled with such temptations. The reverse is true! When he thinks of his servants he thinks of them as fellow-humans, on a par with himself, having God as their Creator just as he does. He feels this way not only about his male servants, that's how he feels about his female servants. In a world that treated women in abysmal fashion, here was one who openly held them in esteem! Listen to him, "If I have denied justice to my menservants and maidservants when they had a grievance against me, what will I do when God confronts me? What will I answer when called to account? Did not he who made me in the womb make them? Did not the same one form us both within our mothers?" (31:13-15).

And he doesn't say this in a pompous way. Under terrible pressure he feels compelled to sketch his character as seen in his past life. He isn't addressing a hostile feminist movement. In the course of his character sketch he mentions how he viewed his female servants. It's a "passing" remark and the more powerful because it isn't a studied statement geared for a particular group to gain its approval. No, money or position hadn't corrupted this man. He remained humble, with a healthy view of everyone around him. He was no god, just another human into whose hands God had given riches and power.

When he approached to take his place in the seat of power in the city square, the young men stepped back and made a path for him. The aged rose from their seats as a token of their respect and the leading lights, the people with the power, even they broke off their speaking when the great man came into their presence (29:7-10). They were anxious to hear him speak and when he spoke, they didn't feel threatened. His words fell gently on their ears and how well he expressed himself, everyone said (29:10-11,21-23). When their debates generated heat but little light, when they stirred up dust and choked one another's minds, his words came, they felt, "like spring rain" that softened the ground after the long cold winter.

Was he powerful? Yes! As they walked the streets they hoped they would see him and if it happened he saw them and gave them a smile, it made their day. "When I smiled at them, they scarcely believed it; the light of my face was precious to them" (29:24). Perhaps you've had a memorable experience when someone who was far above you in office and status made a point of smiling or speaking. Don't you remember how delightful it was? What a lovely thing, what a very lovely thing they do, those who know they have such power, when they brighten the day of people who live most of their lives unnoticed and without applause.

In Thomas Hauser's biography of Muhammad Ali, Harold

Conrad, the boxing promoter, tells of the time he and Ali visited a women's prison in California. Of course the ladies were absolutely beside themselves with joy that this super star would take the time and trouble and they'd get to see him. They were lined up to shake hands with him and get his autograph. Every now and then he would stop to kiss one of them—but let me let Conrad tell the rest:

> And every one he kissed was ugly. The first one he kissed, if they'd had an ugly woman contest, she would have won. He leaned over, hugged her and kissed her, and she just about fainted. She was crying, 'Oh, my God! He kissed me! He kissed me!' Then the next one . . . he kept kissing the ugly ones. Afterward, I asked him why, and he told me, 'The good-looking ones ain't got no problem. But them ugly ones, who's gonna kiss them? If I kiss them, they've got something to talk about for the rest of their lives.'[2]

Ask yourself and reflect on it for a while to appreciate it. How did these women feel as they went back to their cells after he had leaned over and kissed them? Rescued permanently from oblivion and given a lovely memory to bring out and warm themselves on days that are getting too heavy to bear! "Somebody noticed me. Someone took the time. Someone thought about me and my need."

The singer and movie actor, Kris Kristofferson, has a similar story to tell. About taking time for people, Ali once told him: "You don't realize how much it means to these people. A lot of them have never met anybody famous."[3] Then Ali went on to tell him that when he was a little boy his father took him to a tree that Joe Louis had leaned against in Louisville. That was when he first realized how much it could mean to someone to make contact with someone famous.

This is a fine sense of the situation. Neither Ali nor Job was taking himself too seriously. They just knew how lovely it is to be noticed and treated as though they mattered. In moments like these, position and power are being used to good effect. For all his many and serious faults Robert Burns the Scottish national poet never forgot his old friends and his humble beginnings. Even after he had been established as a big celebrity, wined and dined by lords and ladies, he would break off a conversation in the street with some one in the upper echelons to say hello to an old companion. This is one of the reasons he's beloved by Scotsmen to this day. We don't have to be "big wheels" to make a difference as Dave Smoot discovered.

Surgeon Dave Smoot had emergency abdominal surgery and for the first time, he tells us in his August 1987 *Guideposts* article, he knew how it felt to be on the other end of the knife. He learned what it was like to be afraid, looking up instead of down, without control and helpless, scared, tired of being poked, pushed, rolled, humiliated and treated with clinical efficiency.

Close to 6:30 A.M. he tells us the morning shift begins when "one old, squatty, Cabbage Patch doll of a nurse" arrives to go through her paces before heading for the door. He's feeling lonely, vulnerable and the efficiency of it all only adds to his pain. "Then," he says, "she turns around and goes to the sink, moistens a clean washcloth with warm water and quietly wipes my unshaven face. Her only words to me are, 'This must be hard for you.'" Smoot goes on:

> This usually detached, controlled doctor feels his eyes fill with tears. It has been a harsh winter where I live; it has been a harsh night learning the lessons of suffering. Someone I don't even know has taken a moment to acknowledge me as a human being. In this impersonal hospital room, someone has paused to reflect on my feelings, to share my burden with precious, sparse words: "This must be hard for you."

This is power used as it should be used! Away from the public eye this is how Job behaved and when it came to public legal matters, he was the same Job: "If I have raised my hand against the fatherless, knowing that I had influence in court, then let my arm fall from my shoulder, let it be broken off at the joint" (31:21-22).

We've seen in recent times how easy it is for the wealthy and connected to buy themselves out of trouble. We know enough about people in power bending the rules in their own favor. "If I've done that," said this passionate man from Uz. "If I've done that may my arm be ripped from its socket!"

To be secure enough to spurn the crowds, powerful enough to bury your opponents, wealthy enough to buy your judges, popular enough to fix decisions but utterly to refuse to live like that—this is integrity! This is better than money, better than political power. *This is life in the sunlight!*

But there's more, much more. Listen to this: "I was eyes to the blind and feet to the lame. I was a father to the needy; I took up the case of the stranger" (29:15-16). Not only would he not press claims against the defenseless, threatening to take them to court because he knew he'd get his way there, he used his power and influence to get a hearing for the voiceless. When the resident alien came to him in the city square, just inside the gate, he could be sure that Job would take up his case and get him glad-hearted justice as if he were a home-born person. We're not talking here about a frigid impartiality, a cold justice that would freeze salt water. No! This Job was a passionate lover of people who couldn't bear to see them out there on their own. His heart couldn't bear it so he took up their cause and saw it out to the end. (And when he was fighting his own righteous cause it was this same passion for right that drove him to oppose both his friends and God. He never changed. He'd go up against corrupt judges in human courts and he'd go up against God Almighty himself if he thought the cause was just.)

Here was the richest and most powerful man in the whole of the East, apologizing to no one for his wealth and power, refusing to be a prisoner of conscience because he had so much and many others had so little. Here he is, so living his life that, as we reflect on it, we're envious and wish we were like him. His loveliness and not his bank balance measure his greatness. This is a man who could rejoice in his integrity, who could transform lives from misery to glory, who took a personal interest in societal justice, who took advantage of no one and assisted everyone. *That's life in the sunlight!* And that's where the man from Uz lived.

*To be secure enough to spurn the crowds,
powerful enough to bury your opponents,
wealthy enough to buy your judges, popular
enough to fix decisions but utterly to refuse to
live like that—this is integrity! This is better
than money, better than political power.
This is life in the sunlight!*

3
LANCELOT'S LAMENT

"Perhaps the real question should always be, not 'What kind
of wife does she have to be for me to be true to my promises
but what kind of person do I need to be to keep them?'"

James Keenan

Somebody said that prominent people, like politicians and preachers, when they fall, always fall in the areas of power or money or sex. There seems to be a lot of evidence to establish that viewpoint. Thankfully there are those among us who have lived splendidly in the limelight and who remind us that our defeat is no foregone conclusion. Job was one of them. His brave response to life on the ash heap is breathtaking, but his princely response to life in the midst of success was glorious. To be true to the basic relationships and commitments in life is the kind of thing that turns God's head.

And faithfulness to those basic relationships has its spin-off rewards. For one thing, when we do what's right, we don't have to lament as Lancelot did. In Tennyson's Arthurian legends no one was greater than Lancelot. Knight of knights, bravest of the brave, defender of the defenseless, fearless righter of wrongs, unbeatable warrior, sunny in disposition, known from one end of the kingdom to the other, daydream of countless young women's' hearts *and sinner with another man's wife!*

At one point in his royal career Lancelot was badly wounded and young Elaine nursed him from the point of death until he fully recovered, falling in love with him in the course of the matter. Because her love for him was so deep and so tender, and because he is so enamored with Guinevere, and because he wants Elaine to think less of him and forget him—because all this is true, Lancelot rides off in pretended indifference, without a word to the girl who had done so much for him.

In her despair and loneliness she kills herself. Lancelot is in agony when he hears it and his guilty heart links this great wrong and his own great wrong with Guinevere. King Arthur, the only man in the kingdom who *doesn't* know something is wrong, is telling Lancelot how wonderful he is and how wonderful it is that such a girl could love him so deeply. But the sinner can bear to hear no more praise and leaves to walk down by the river, where he expresses his self-hatred and the pain he brings to everyone around him.

> For what am I? What profits me my name
>   of greatest knight?
> I fought for it, and have it:
> Pleasure to have it, none; to lose it, pain;
> Now grown a part of me: but what use is it?
> To make men worse by making my sin known?
> Or sin seem less, the sinner seeming great?[4]

He tells himself he has become used to having this wondrous reputation but finds no pleasure in it, though it would give him pain to lose it. Under God he has become a household word, people swear by his name and take him as their model for life. But because of his sin, his fame will weaken men's hearts. Precisely because he has such fame, precisely because everyone is looking to him, the story of his shame will spread the farther and discourage the more, disappoint the more, make cynical the more.

Or, maybe even worse! When men see someone as valiant and good as Lancelot involved in such an evil, will they not think the evil isn't so bad? Might they not dismiss the horror of the wrong because they are blinded by this man's greatness? ("Well, when you're as great as Lancelot, people have to make allowances. . . .")

Where Lancelot fell many a great man or woman has fallen. Now in the position where they can help people most, they hurt them. God having given them the ears and the eyes of the people they "make men worse by making their sin known or sin seem less, the sinner seeming great."

But it wasn't so with the man from Uz. This was no lecherous old man who eyed the girls or made moves on another man's wife. Not only did he not do what was wicked, he even covenanted with his heart not to *think* what was wicked. We need to remember that what Jesus said in Matthew 5:27-28 wasn't new and that the full will of God was already available to Job's peers who had narrowed it down to suit them. Here's what he says in 31:1,9-11:

> I made a covenant with my eyes not to look lustfully at a girl . . . If my heart has been enticed by a woman, or if I have lurked at my neighbor's door, then may my wife grind another man's grain, and may other men sleep with her. For that would have been shameful, a sin to be judged.

He who couldn't stand to see widows in need or orphans destitute and alone, who couldn't bear to see the poor be hungry or cold, who wouldn't dream of using his powerful position at the court against anyone—he kept himself for the one woman with whom he made a covenant of marriage! Was there ever such a glorious life as this man's? Is it any wonder God's eyes shone with admiration when he thought of him?

God and Job both knew he was a sinner. He says this in his own defense, "If I have concealed my sin as men do, by hiding my sin in my heart because I so feared the crowd and so dreaded the contempt of the clans that I kept silent and would not go outside. . . ." (31:33-34). He takes it for granted that they know he is a sinner but his sin didn't characterize his life, it was the goodness of God in it that best described him. His life was an open book, he rejoiced in what was noble and compassionate and that's how he had been since boyhood (31:18). And he was true to his wife!

And for all the talk of a sexual revolution, for all the talk of our sexual freedom that says we should do "away with Victorian prudishness," marital faithfulness is alive and well, still highly prized and sought after. To look at a wife or husband whose joy in life includes the rich satisfaction of knowing (without thinking about it too much) that they have kept faith with God and someone else at a profound level—to look at such a person is to see one of God's truly great creations. Let those sneer that want to but it isn't joyous and warm righteous loyalty that's on trial here; it's the shabby behavior of the poor gutless fool who hasn't it in her/him to keep her/his pledged word.

And listen, millions live together in marital contentment, who not only don't have affairs, they don't even *think* of them. They're too pleased with married life as it is, too pleased with life out in the sunlight that they wouldn't dream of slinking around in the dark.

To live with guilty secrets; to be afraid that others will discover; to feel awkward in the company of someone who cannot keep from praising you, who trusts you—to look at your unsuspecting children, at his or hers; to be so ashamed that you can't engage in noble ventures that need your help lest you bring them into disrepute should the truth come out—*to live like that is to live in the shadows*. Those of us who know what it is to have behaved shamefully know beyond debate that no amount of money, power, or praise can make a sordid life sunny!

To love one with no wish to love another; to keep your covenant cheerfully in the face of other influences; to lie beside that one and that one only in the gentle darkness is to live in the sunlight. No degree of poverty, no business failure, no being aware that we didn't "make our mark in this life" can take that away or obliterate the luster of a life like that, or fill it with unbroken gloom. To avoid not only the deed but also the sinister longing, the wishing, now *that's* integrity. Job and millions of others made a lifelong practice of what F.W Robertson spoke about when he said:

> Beware of those fancies, those day dreams, which represent things as possible which should be forever impossible. Beware of that affection which cares for your happiness more than for your honor.[5]

> The man from Uz lived a vibrant, joyous life
> of passionate integrity and loyalty to his wife
> and children. Isn't love grand? That's life in the
> sunshine; that's bringing God glory and praise!

4

THE JOY OF LIVING

"There, in the presence of the LORD your God, you and your families shall eat and shall rejoice in everything you have put your hand to, because the LORD your God has blessed you."

Deuteronomy 12:7

Richard Dreyfuss and Bill Murray starred in the truly funny comedy *What About Bob?* Dreyfuss is a psychiatrist who is driven insane by a nutty patient (Murray) who, believe it or not, ends up curing the professor's neurotic family on his way to driving the doctor mad. The psychiatrist is an (almost lovable) impatient control freak whose talent is about to be rewarded when *Good Morning America* is scheduled to interview him about his new book, *Baby Steps*.

Murray (who unnerved me as much as he did the screen doctor) arrives at Dreyfuss's holiday home, ingratiates himself with his family, and ends up eating with them at a family meal while the doctor foams at the mouth in despair and rage. As he forks creamed potatoes into his mouth the patient moans with delight, as he bites into more fried chicken he rolls his eyes in ecstasy, as he downs one more roll he wrinkles his face with sheer pleasure. The doctor enjoys nothing, scowling at everything while the visitor is alive to everything.

You can guess how the visitor's open and vocal delight with the food thrilled the two children and the mother who all worked to get the meal together. I wish I could spell the sounds he was making as he spread sunshine to every corner of the room (except to the end of the table, where the poor miserable doctor was sitting). "Mmmmm, Mmmm" he'd moan as he put more food in mouth before he was quite finished with what was already in there. And when they asked him if he wanted more, of course he did!

For all his hang-ups, Bob was living life to the full, tasting every delicious morsel, and wanting his plate replenished. ("Pile it high and deep," he says at one point.) The mother and kids were thrilled with his response and delighted to have him around, and no wonder. It was only the poor sourpuss dad who was losing out on the life that was happening there right in front of his out-of-joint nose. And don't you think God himself is pleased with that kind of response to his outpoured blessings? He not only loves a cheerful giver, he smiles at joyous receivers like Bob who have creamed potatoes all over their faces and fried chicken half in and half out of their mouths while their mmmming and ummming all over the place.

I take it Job was an older man since he contrasts himself with the young, but not too old since he speaks of the aged as a separate group (29:8). The slice of his life the book is mainly concerned with is the pain-filled period of loss and mental agony that fell on him in his later years. But that period wasn't all there was to Job's life. The bulk of it was lived in the sunshine even though he knew from personal contact that there were many who lived in dire need. He speaks of his pre-calamity days as days of pleasure, filled with joy and peace, before, with and from God.

It won't hurt us to emphasize this since it's easy to give the impression that the book of Job presents the world as one bleak, pitiless, joyless piece of rock flying round and round like an Alcatraz in space. There's more to living than dying! There's more to glorious living than struggling nobly in the coils of some mind-bending tragedy and the book of Job makes that clear to us.

You don't have to be a genius or a seer to recognize the awful pain in the lives of millions, but it takes balance to keep from completely agreeing with Aldonza's view of reality: "The world's a dung heap and we're all maggots crawling on top of it." (You might remember she was the kitchen trollop in the movie *The Man of La Mancha*.)

It isn't hard to understand how a crushing loss would keep us from a full-orbed vision of things. Nor does it surprise us if prolonged suffering makes our friends forget that they had years of peace and joy before the knife went deep to their hearts. None of this requires explanation or whispered apologies from the sufferers.

Still, gloom and despair are not the only responses to suffering as we can see and hear from ten thousand times ten thousand sufferers down the ages. That multitudes rise above their pain and through their pain find life to be deeper and richer than they dreamed doesn't mean other poor souls don't go down under their burdens; it doesn't mean we don't work to ease the pain of others. Of course not. Only a fool, an insensitive clod, dismisses the agony and loneliness of the vast crowd on earth.

Ralph Waldo Emerson's optimism is said to have absolutely scunnered Goethe and maybe Emerson *was* a bit over the top. This fixed-smile approach to life is hard to stomach, but the sour, crabby, gloomy attitude toward life is no cure for naive optimism and it isn't much help to the sufferers, or those who care for them.

You wonder about biblical scholars who make a career out of spreading gloom and tirelessly calling others to see the pain in life as if they were the only ones who knew what was going on in the world; as if tragedy were the only reality in the world. One Old Testament scholar loves to pour it on. In a critical review of a colleague's book he implied its author was afraid to hear the truth about life and that he didn't take the horrors of life seriously enough. He said he preferred Job's view of life to the author's. Of course, he was speaking of Job's view of life while he was under the awful agony of loss.

But this is as one-sided as he claimed others were being. In the pre- and post-calamity Job thought life was wonderful. You have to glibly dismiss the joyful parts of his life if you wish to maintain the snarling and gloomy stance. True enough, the tough phase of Job's life gets the lion's share of the text but that doesn't mean we're to obliterate the rest, and it certainly doesn't mean we should forget that the bulk of his life was filled with joy and praise for God. Paul Scherer was on target with some of us when he said:

> If what a man sees is monstrous, hate not love, ugliness not beauty, gloom not gladness, the chances are that he is staring in a mirror at his own image. It is not just the life around him, it is the life within that calls for a cleansing, healing touch. In Dickens's *Christmas Carol* Christmas had not changed; Scrooge had, and more than once.[6]

Since the Old Testament scholar I have in mind has dismissed the normative teaching of the whole biblical canon and can no longer believe, so he says, in life after death, maybe it's hardly surprising that he speaks with a sneer and writes words that sound like a death march. Meanwhile, Job longed for the pre-calamity days when he thrilled to each new morning with its family pleasures, its social joys and its opportunities to help the needy (29:4-25). He didn't apologize for missing those days. They were wonderful, why wouldn't he miss them? And we can picture him in his post-calamity days spinning around in ecstasy like Snoopy in a *Peanuts* cartoon, enjoying a wonderful life and praising God for all his goodness. Like Bob he probably wolfed down his fried chicken with pleasure-filled groans and asked for second helpings of salad ("Pile them high and deep," he might have said).

Sometimes it isn't agony or "all the facts" that gives us a jaundiced eye—sometimes it's boredom and loss of faith. It might even be sophisticated ingratitude; an ingratitude that gives intelligent reasons for being thankless, that offers scholarly reasons for gracelessly dismissing the joys of life, that parades morbid arguments, that quenches the praise of God in other contented hearts. (See 15:4 where Job is accused of undermining devotion to God. Job we know, but who are these non-suffering, bored and boring cynics?)

God bless all those hearts that have been broken into a thousand pieces and turned every fragment into a prayer that scorns pessimism. God bless all those who know how to glorify him in their abundance; those who make God smile by the way they eat their food, and wrestle with their kids and flirt with their wives/husbands. God bless all the boys and girls who know that romantic love is a gift of God that they not only should enjoy in honor but who know they should *enjoy* it! God bless all those whose faith gives them eyes to see even the *hidden* depths of calamities and who cheerfully run to assist those who are burdened by them. And in helping, they make it clear that the sun still shines in a world where there's too much darkness. Whatever adjustments need to be made and *will* be made by God, this *is* the world of the God and Father of our Lord Jesus Christ and the last word is with life not death, with gladness not gloom, with praise and not protest.

5

WITH HELP FROM FRED AND GINGER

"The world cannot be wrong,
If in this world there's you."

Charlie Chaplin

What P.T. Forsyth said is no doubt true. He said human loves are a gift from God but they aren't the same as soon as they leave God's hand and we receive them. I'm certain he's right, but they aren't so corrupted that they're no longer his gifts and they aren't always so perverted as to be unrecognizable. Human loves whether they are romantic, familial, or friendship experiences are to be treasured and rejoiced in. Not worshiped; not made an end in themselves nor thought to be the answers to our most basic needs but enjoyed just the same!

Hollywood hasn't done us a lot of favors in its movie making in the last number of years but my suspicion is that Christians have had too little to say in favor of romance. We don't mind praising love between family members or friends but when it comes to romance we either play it down or think talking about it publicly is somehow suspect because after all, it's "agape" that really counts. When we do talk about it we go out of our way to show how it could fit in with a Christian outlook. We find the Song of Solomon a bit spicy, maybe even a bit embarrassing (what's it doing in the Bible anyway—a book like that?). Romantic love doesn't seem to be quite religious enough so we have to baptize it. I'm convinced we should remind ourselves that all aspects of our lives should be lived for God and in his sight but the things God gives us are to be enjoyed! There's nothing shameful in romance and maybe if we didn't leave it all to Hollywood we would have less to be embarrassed about. If Ecclesiastes teaches us anything we can agree on it's this: enjoy what

God has given you beneath the sun. People who tell you that honorable romance isn't a blessing from God that can help you live a Christian life to the full aren't fully awake. Let's be done with the "Bah, humbug!" approach to romantic love and enjoy ourselves.

You don't have to be a poet or songwriter to know what Irving Berlin was driving at when he had Fred Astaire singing "Isn't This a Lovely Day to Be Caught in the Rain?" to Ginger Rogers. You might remember that Fred had lost his heart to Ginger who was giving him the big freeze—well, not too big a freeze. She goes horseback riding and ends up in the park during a terrible storm at which point Fred arrives to keep her company and to give her his view of the situation. There are at least two ways to be caught out in miserable weather. By yourself or with someone you're crazy about. Being with someone whose presence pleases you makes a difficult situation a lot better than tolerable. Here's how Fred puts it to Ginger before their feet began to tap out agreement:

> The weather is frightening.
> The thunder and lightning
> Seem to be having their way.
> But as far as I'm concerned it's a lovely day.
>
> The turn in the weather
> Can keep us together
> So that I can honestly say
> That as far as I'm concerned it's a lovely day.
>
> And everything's okay.
> Isn't this a lovely day to be caught in the rain?
> You were going on your way now you've got to remain.
> Just when you were going leaving me all at sea,
> The clouds broke, they broke,
> And oh what a break for me.
>
> I can see the sun up high
> Though we're caught in a storm.
> I can see where you and I could be cozy and warm;
> Let the rain go pitter patter, it really doesn't matter
> If skies are gray
> As long as I can be with you,
> It's a lovely day.[7]

At the surface level of life millions of us have been lucky enough to know how it feels to be "singing in the rain." The picnic that was a washout, the restaurant that was packed out and the article that was rejected—but "as long as I can be with you, it's a lovely day." There was the freezing night when the storm cut off the power and the kids slept with you "cozy and warm." The busted plumbing and the flooded kitchen, the car breaking down on a long stretch of road between towns, the motel reservation they knew nothing about or the long night trying to sleep in the airport; these and ten thousand other non-life-threatening situations shared with someone who made it possible to see a brighter side of things are part of what makes you contented when both of you have lived out a full life and lay your tired bodies down. To have someone who makes that true for you is no small gift from God. To *be* someone like that—now that's some privilege, and power.

It isn't a good thing to attempt to bear *everyone's* burdens. In any case, it isn't possible. Just the same, it's fine and right to make things easier for people within reach of us and if we can't remove the difficulties, at last we can work to make the playing field level for as many as possible. If we can't do it for everyone, we can do it for some; if we can't do it for many we can do it for a few. And because we can't do it for many, does that excuse us from doing it for a few?

So, give her reason to feel you're the kind of person she likes to have around in a storm. Give him reason to be grateful if it was hard times that drove you together. Tell her why it's a lovely day when you're with her, even when the miseries seem to have everything going for them. We aren't all brimful of courage but we can be kind, cheerful, affirming, even thankful. It's amazing how somebody's simple thankfulness brightens a day. I don't mean groveling, or a syrupy gratitude that's too sweet to be wholesome. I'm talking about a healthy, unashamed capacity to recognize when we've been helped and a willingness to let it show. What's she got that takes the misery out of a murky day? What's she got that helps you to see the sun even in a torrential downpour?

Figure it out, rejoice in it and, if you're up to it (and not all of us are), tap dance your way around her, singing, "Let the rain pitter patter; it really doesn't matter if skies are gray; As long as I can be with you it's a lovely day."

*E*ach will be like a hiding place from the wind, a covert
from the tempest, like streams of water in a dry place,
like the shade of a great rock in a weary land.

Isaiah 32:2 NRSV

6

WRITE HER A NOTE

"Your last letter should have been written in light on
hummingbird's wings. It is love o'erfused with air.
To be loved by you is all in all. . . ."
Harold (a hospital patient to his beloved)

Poor Alexander Pope! A tubercular disease twisted his spine
and left him hunch-backed, spindly-legged, four-foot-six-inches
tall and terribly sensitive to cold. Completely dependent on others
on rising and going to bed, dressing and getting seated; he had to
wear laced-up canvas corsets for uprightness, flannel shirts and
waistcoats for heat and three pairs of socks to make his spidery
legs look something like normal. But did anyone ever put more literary genius into writing *anything* than he put into writing things
that tore and wounded and insulted and humiliated?

Of course he wrote in the 18th century, which Henry Thomas
said was an age accustomed to slugging below the belt with brass-
bound knuckles. Besides, the poet Dennis called him a "hunch-
back'd toad" and, so it is said—when he offered himself as a suit-
or to Lady Mary Montagu who was delighted with his wit and
charm—when he did that, she patted his dear little head and,
unable to keep from it, broke into a bout of laughing and nearly fell
off her seat. The fury of a scorned woman is one thing but—. Can
you imagine how deeply that must have gouged him? In the loneliness of his room did he look in the mirror and curse his image
and steel himself for ruthless verbal revenge? Well, with one thing
or another he became, as he himself insisted, the most feared,
because the most skilfully savage, man in England. He wrote:

Yes, I am proud; and must be proud, to see
Men not afraid of God afraid of me.

It didn't matter that the same could be said of mad dogs, angry wasps or voracious parasites. Still, his genius wasn't confined to writing insults nor was he alone in it. The famous Samuel Johnson said of Thomas Sheridan, "Why, Sir, Sherry is dull, naturally dull; but it must have taken him a great deal of pains to become what we now see him. Such excess of stupidity, Sir, is not in nature." Thomas Carlyle called Milne's biography of the poet John Keats, "Fricassee of dead dog" and a writer for the *Quarterly Review* wrote of literary critic William Hazlitt in these terms: "A mere ulcer; a sore from head to foot; a poor devil so completely flayed that there is not a square inch of healthy flesh on his carcass; an overgrown pimple, sore to the touch."

Not all of it was so brutal. Melville, the author of *Moby Dick* remarked on Ralph Waldo Emerson's self-confidence that "had he lived in those days when the world was made, he might have offered some valuable suggestions." And Sidney Smith said to the endlessly chattering Lord Macaulay, "You know, when I am gone you will be sorry you never heard me speak." In later years, despite exceptions, the insults were usually less venomous and more sophisticated. Oscar Wilde, speaking of Dickens's *Old Curiosity Shop* said, "One must have a heart of stone to read the death of little Nell without laughing" and Mark Twain would say, "Wagner's music is better than it sounds." Literary critic, Israel Zangwill, noted about G.B. Shaw, "The way Bernard Shaw believes in himself is very refreshing in these atheistic days when so many people believe in no God at all."

Enough of that! It isn't necessary for us to be as foul-mouthed in our letter writing as D.H. Lawrence could be or as crude as Robbie Burns in some of his poetry. There's enough in the world that's warm, earthy, genuine and tender to point the direction that in our better moments we want to go. And there are enough people in the world who need us to tell them something of another kind.

Job thought his friends were "miserable comforters" whose long-windedness drove him wild (16:2-3). He was on the rack and they were using words like battering rams (16:4). He knew in his own heart that if the roles were reversed that "my mouth would encourage you; comfort from my lips would bring you relief" (16:5). It is well known (or he wouldn't have said so) that when he spoke he spoke wisely and gently (29:22). And because that was true of him he not unreasonably expected it to be true of his friends, especially now, when he was on the edge of the abyss. They would have been better friends to him and more helpful if they had been kind and encouraging rather than long-winded in their criticism.

Arthur Gordon in that marvelous way of his made that point. His mother was moving out of her home down in Georgia where her family had lived for nearly a century and a half. He and his sisters went down to check out the "stuff" that had accumulated. The attic and cellar were crammed with boxes and trunks of stuff and Arthur was hoping to find some rare stamps or the signature of some famous person. He found letters.

No scandals, no grand chronicle of historic events, no passionate love letters. None of that, but in letter after letter he read unashamed love and admiration expressed for someone or other. "You don't know how much your visit meant to each of us! When you left, I felt as if the sun had stopped shining." "Never forget how much your friends and family love and admire you." "How wonderful you are."

Gordon saw his own generation as having drifted from that kind of speech. (The famous broadcaster A.L. Alexander agreed with Gordon's assessment of the new trend.) It had become corny, a bit too gushy for a tough generation, I suppose. Whatever the reason, he's right when he says the change "seriously interferes with one of the deepest of all human needs—the desire for acceptance and approval by other people."

But though his own "tough" generation might have thought warm tender speech was corny, he reminds us that those who wrote the letters he found in that old house had been through their own tough war that brought defeat, poverty and humiliation. They faced their tough times with great fortitude and strength; and where did they get it? Gordon tells us: "The answer lay in my dusty hands. They got it from each other."

So write her a note. Tell her you love her. It doesn't have to be a fancy card. Might even be better if it isn't a fancy card. A napkin from a restaurant, a paper towel in your motel room—anything that lets you scrawl some word of love from your heart to hers. An "anonymous" love letter that subtly lets the cat out of the bag about who wrote it. She'll call you silly when she sees it but she'll store it away somewhere to look at again and again, and smile, and tell herself how silly you are.

If you've seen the movie *The Man of La Mancha* you might remember that Don Quixote sent a note by his friend Sancho

Panza to Aldonza whom the mad knight thinks is his Lady Dulcinea (or should I say the note is to his Lady Dulcinea who thinks she's Aldonza?). The squire tells the kitchen trollop why he's there and she, because she can't read, tells him to read while she's wolfing down a meal. The words are grand and lovely—too grand and lovely for her—so she keeps mocking and protesting. Still, though she's not in the least interested (of course!), she insists that he keep reading. When he's done and is turning to leave, the coarse, rude and mocking woman grabs the note—not that she's interested, you understand. Sancho leaves and Aldonza takes the note out of her pocket and with a softened look scans the ink marks that mean all the lovely things he'd said to her. People love to get lovely notes, even if they think they're too grand. Write her a note and tell her how fine she is to you.

Let the words be your own, let your own heart speak with its own voice and so maintain its integrity. Let them be "romantic" without confining them only to romantic phrases. What is there about her that warms you when you're cold, gives you strength when you're weak or that comforts you when you feel you're all alone? Tell her about those things. By all means, tell her she's "a pretty face" but tell her she's more than that. Tell her she drives you wild with desire if that's what the situation calls for, but tell her it goes deeper than all that, it's more lasting than that. Tell her what you feel for her is fed by beauty she has that will be there when her physical beauty is fading or long gone.

There's something magical about words but writing has a magic of its own. It's no substitute for unwritten speech, but there's something special about pieces of paper that are enchanted, that are covered with life-transforming squiggles and sprawlings. There are ten thousand times ten thousand and thousands of thousands sheets or bits of paper but these are special because a heart poured out the kind things that create a new and brighter world for someone. Long after the writer and the beloved are gone, they still have their magical power.

Some years ago while plundering to find an old picture I had an Arthur Gordon experience of my own. I came across *scores* of letters and cards I had written to Ethel—there they were, in a couple of old purses and in a large cookie tin. I didn't know she'd kept them. I began to read them and must have read for more than an hour, stopping to reflect on the times, places and circumstances, trying to reconstruct the original settings. A lot of it was chit-chat and local news but much of it was tender, grateful and warm. Some of it ached with loneliness and so I knew if I'd been feeling like that at times Ethel had too. I want to leave some more letters lying around after I'm gone.

When you think of how many ugly things have found their way into print, wouldn't it be lovely to pour your own cup of sweetness into the ocean of finely written things. Give her (or him or them) the chance to bring it out every now and then to take pleasure in its softness and tenderness, its generosity and assurance. Don't let anyone persuade you that the "ordinary" kindnesses of life are ordinary. They're not! Don't let anyone persuade you—least of all me—that the only way you can please and praise God is to wrestle gallantly with profound sorrow; it isn't so. You can do what Job did long before the sky fell in on him, spill ordinary words and deeds of sunshine all over creation.

And do you know what God will do? He'll turn to some adversary of his and say, "Have you considered my servant—?"

Now, where's that pen of mine?

There's something magical about words but writing has a magic of its own. It's no substitute for unwritten speech, but there's something special about pieces of paper that are enchanted, that are covered with life-transforming squiggles and sprawlings. There are ten thousand times ten thousand and thousands of thousands sheets or bits of paper but these are special because a heart poured out the kind things that create a new and brighter world for someone. Long after the writer and the beloved are gone, they still have their magical power.

7

CALLING A GREEN LEAF GRAY

"The LORD gave and the LORD has taken away...."

Job 1:21

"Shall we accept good from God, and not trouble?"

Job 2:10

Gilbert K. Chesterton was heading for a nervous breakdown and I suppose it didn't help that he was reading the book of Ecclesiastes. If you're in the wrong frame of mind that book just might complete your journey toward one. Well, what are we to say of a book that opens with this (1:2), "'Meaningless! Meaningless!' says the Teacher. 'Utterly meaningless! Everything is meaningless!'" Chesterton, like so many of us, didn't understand the thrust of the book but he knew he didn't like it so he wrote a poem protesting its message. He called the poem *Ecclesiastes*. Here's how it goes:

> There is one sin: to call a green leaf grey,
> Whereat the sun in heaven shuddereth.
> There is one blasphemy: for death to pray,
> For God alone knoweth the praise of death.
> There is one creed: 'neath no world-terror's wing
> Apples forget to grow on apple-trees.
> There is one thing needful—everything—
> The rest is vanity of vanities.

The book of Ecclesiastes speaks its own truth in its own way but so does Chesterton's poem. The Englishman was a lover of life and he gladly embraced it all. He resisted gloom and while he admitted there were horrors in life he took life in its fullness because, along with his temperament, he trusted in a God who not only knew what was going on but was at work in it all. That was enough for Chesterton. And until the preachers confused Job (beginning in chapter 4) it was enough for Job.

There's little doubt that the loss of family, wealth and all that goes with that depressed Job to the brink of despair but we're not to think he had a faith crisis for that reason. His rage and unbridled speech didn't begin with the loss of his prosperity—it began with the loss of his divine Friend. When he makes his "oath of innocence" he can't hold back the longing for the days when God and he were on good terms. "Oh, for the days when I was in my prime, when God's intimate friendship blessed my house, when the Almighty was still with me. . . ." (29:4-5). What enraged him was the thought that his Friend had turned from him and was accusing him (Job) of having been faithless.

Job was willing to live life in the sunshine or on the ash heap as long as he had God. The Lord "gave" he said, and how richly he had given, so how could he be ungrateful? The Lord took away. So it was Job's turn to experience sorrow and loss. If that's how the Lord willed it, he was content to accept that. For years he had received good from the Lord and now it was time to bear the trouble. ". . . the name of the LORD be praised," he said (1:21). It's a bit disappointing after a while to hear his gloom in chapter three, but then again maybe it shouldn't surprise us.

To be depressed in great trouble is one thing, to have a sour heart is something else. To groan in pain is understandable, to look at life with a jaundiced eye is something else. Christ didn't say, "Blessed are the moaners." To dismiss the heartache as if it were non-living and embrace only the pleasant in life is not only to be ungrateful, it's self-centered. Is God only God when things are going our way? Does God care only when our lives are running smoothly and pleasantly? It's one thing for our emotional state to change, it's something else for our theology to be tossed aside because we're down in the mouth. Do we believe that God cared for Job and for Jesus Christ when they were going through their sore times? Maybe God has his own purposes in the trouble as well as in the pleasant.

"There is one thing needful," says Chesterton. "Everything!" The rest is meaningless. To believe that God is doing glorious things every day without fail and that he is moving his creation to a glorious finale makes it clear that no matter what world-terror has spread its wings like a giant vulture over the entire world, apples will still grow on apple trees. Look out your window, says the poet, see if the sun's still shining, see if the children are still playing, make sure apple trees still bring apples. If all this is true then it's a sin to call a gloriously green leaf gray. There are troubles that beggar description in the lives of many people and I've no wish to describe them, much less dismiss them, but God will fully justify himself one of these days and has given us full assurance of that in the cross of Christ. So with the man of Uz we will say,

"The LORD gave and the LORD has taken away; praise
the LORD" and refuse to call a single green leaf gray.

One woman who stands and defies an evil world is a redeemer. One boy or girl who will not bow to the shabby standards that a host of kids pay homage to is a savior. Just by living they say, "If there's one there can be a thousand and if there's a thousand there can be a million and if there's a million there can be a world full." But perhaps equally inspiring they say, "However many there'll be, by God's grace there'll be one!"

8

THE PROPHETIC NATURE
OF A LOVELY LIFE

"Can a mortal man be more righteous than God?
Can a man be more pure than his Maker?"

Job 4:17

To watch a man live as Job lived is an incredible lift to the soul. Since the world around us is so full of wickedness and since we're so often disappointed and occasionally devastated to silence by the wickedness within us, we can easily begin to believe goodness is completely unattainable or only shows up occasionally. People like Job who are warm as well as upright, who are kind as well as straight—such people make us believe goodness is possible even for us. At least they keep us from sinking without trace because they are one consistently bright and shining light that all the gloom and selfishness of this world can't put out.

One woman who stands and defies an evil world is a redeemer. One boy or girl who will not bow to the shabby standards that a host of kids pay homage to is a savior. Just by living they say, "If there's one there can be a thousand and if there's a thousand there can be a million and if there's a million there can be a world full." But perhaps equally inspiring they say, "However many there'll be, by God's grace there'll be *one*!"

There's something like that in Isaiah 32:1-2 where the prophet speaks of the glorious transformation of society. Not only will leaders rule in righteousness but, "Each man will be like a shelter from the wind and a refuge from the storm, like streams of water in the desert and the shadow of a great rock in a thirsty land." Is there imagery more pleasing than that about the blessing good people are to others? Wordsworth has somewhere said that what a great person does for us is to do what hasn't been done before and in doing it sets a standard for us beneath which we are never content. Men and women, boys and girls like that are our national treasure and security. It isn't a balanced budget, military supremacy or a chicken in every pot that assures our future. It's people who pay homage to a righteousness without which none of us is safe or well. All that is encouraging enough but these people offer us more than that.

Job's friend Eliphaz must have been shocked at the flat, soulless words that poured from Job in gloomy chapter three. He gently reminds Job that he needs to be brave and live up to the words with which he helped others (4:4-5). He's sure that Job has wandered from God but he's also sure that it isn't characteristic of Job, whose life has been one of goodness and nobility (4:6-7). This means Job won't be on the ash heap forever (4:7). Still, having heard Job's depressed and truculent outburst he feels the need to convict Job of sin and so he says, "Can a mortal be more righteous than God? Can a man be more pure than his Maker?" (4:17). He isn't being brutal with him at this point because, he says, it isn't surprising that humans falter now and then (4:18-19). The upshot of all this is that Eliphaz wants Job to repent of his sin and things will turn out all right (5:8,17-18,27) so 4:17, while it's certainly aimed at convicting Job of sin, it does it in a fine way. It's as if he said, "Well of course you've sinned. Compared with God we all fall far short and right now it's your sin that has underlined that truth."

Should we take "righteous" in 4:17 to mean what we usually mean by "justice" or is it "faithfulness"? In the Old Testament the Hebrew word may mean either. In any case, I'm wanting to take up the point Eliphaz clearly makes (following the NIV, KJV and others). If humans are good God is better, if humans are just God is more so, if humans are faithful God is more faithful. No one out-serves, out-fulfills, out-gives or out-lives God!

This means that the sight of a gracious person says things about God. Can a mortal man be more gracious than God? Can a mortal woman be more gallant than God? Will humans give more, stay longer, go farther, stoop lower, climb higher, love more deeply or surpass their holy Father in any way at all? Eliphaz and we are on sure grounds here; God isn't only stronger than we are, he's infinitely better in all the ways that truly count as "greatness"! Those who live sunny lives proclaim truth about a God who is warm and bright and faithful. Can they do something more wonderful for us than that? It would be hard to say what.

III
LIFE IN THE SHADOWS

The book is not about competing systems of moral retribution. It is not about having the courage to call established doctrines in question. It is not about having the faith to doubt. It is not about why good people get hurt. All of these things are touched on in one way or another but whatever Job and his friends are doing or meaning the point always is: Is the man essentially and truly a person of righteousness and integrity?

9

SETTING THE SCENE

"Then the LORD said to Satan, 'Have
you considered my servant Job?'"

Job 2:3

Many scholars are sure that the prose narrative of chapters 1–2 and 42 was written by someone other than the poet who wrote the poem (chapters 3–41). The poet then took an already existing story and used it as a prologue and epilogue to frame his poem. I'm going to take it that if the poet did that he knew what he was doing and that he fitted the borrowed material to his poem. This would mean that the prologue should be taken seriously and allowed to shape our understanding of what is going on in the "dialogues." "After this Job opened his mouth and cursed the day of his birth" (3:1) makes more sense if it is logically connected to the calamities of chapters 1 and 2. So it's not as if the prose material is only the binding that holds the book together. Bildad specifically mentions the death of Job's children (8:4) and repeatedly there are allusions to Job's experiences in chapters 1 and 2. Without the opening chapters, one doesn't know who the disfigured man is that is sobbing and raging against his friends and against heaven. Without the prose, the book isn't the *whole* book.

With that in mind what we're offered is a hero, a central figure about whom a number of things are clearly true.

- His calamities come not because he has sinned but because he has lived so well.
- His troubles come not because God is angry with him but because God is pleased with and proud of him.
- His calamities fell on him not because he was unrighteous but because he was blessedly righteous.

- In taking his blessings from him God is not punishing Job he is putting his trust in him.
- God refuses to speak to him for the same reason.
- For the very same reason God will not explain what has happened and what he is doing.
- God trusted the Job who lived in the sunshine and he trusted the Job who writhed in pain in the shadow.
- He trusted the Job who worshiped and obeyed him and he trusted the Job who accused him of injustice and made the ash heap a shrine of protest.

The whole book shows how Job's righteousness works itself out as he opposes radical suffering, deep depression, unfriendly friends and God himself. This is what happens in the visible realm and at one level. Unknown to Job he is exposing Satan for the cynical creature he is and justifying God's pleasure in him.

No matter how the "dialogues" are conducted and no matter how ragged the nerves of Job and his friends we shouldn't lose sight of the competing claims of Satan and God that trigger the whole spectacle. The book is not about competing systems of moral retribution. It is not about having the courage to call established doctrines in question. It is not about having the faith to doubt. It is not about why good people get hurt. All of these things are touched on in one way or another but whatever Job and his friends are doing or meaning the point always is: Is the man essentially and truly a person of righteousness and integrity? In a sense the book might have closed at 2:10 when Job without resentment allows the Sovereign to be sovereign and take from him all his blessings.

Job does not doubt the existence of moral retribution (he holds that all the way through the exchanges with his friends). Job does not doubt that God is the one who brought the calamities on him (even the narrator insists on that truth). Job does not doubt that God has the right to withdraw the blessings he alone can give. So what's all his angry protest about? Job denied God's right to withdraw the blessings *as punishment for transgressions* when he knew that Job was innocent of any such crimes. But what has all this to do with Satan's accusation against Job? Perhaps we're supposed to understand that Job's loss of family, wealth and health are only part of the loss. He didn't confront those losses with stoic resignation (does chapter 3 sound as if he is a Stoic?), he embraced them like the man of God he was and proved the sincerity of his commitment to God. What was the finest thing Job could do for God before the eyes of the world when the sky fell on him? He did it! Was the loss difficult to take? Was there anything more difficult than experiencing the loss itself? My guess is it was even more difficult to look at the ruins of his life and then say something like, "He is the Lord, let him do what is good in his eyes." But that's what he did! That was his most glorious gift to God—his *trust*.

His humble submission was the stark revelation of his integrity. And the humble submission is all the more glorious because it comes from a man of profound piety, goodness and social generosity. The pain and sense of devastation was almost literally unbearable so chapter 3 functions to make the submission of 1:21 and 2:10 all the more profoundly heroic. Chapter 3 redeems the man from the charge that he was an unfeeling monster. A Stoic? This man was light years away from Stoicism. He felt too deeply, loved too earnestly, devoted himself too purely to God, his family and the world around him to be able to shrug off his losses as if they were nothing. If he'd been able to shrug them off as nothing he would not have been the glorious human with whom God was so pleased.

And what did his friends make of his most glorious gift to God? They trashed it! Instead of hugging him in profound gratitude for his devotion to God they call him to repent of his wickedness against God. They would rob him of the only thing left to him and make of him a vile transgressor. There was nothing he could do to keep from losing the other precious things but no one was going to rob him of what he prized above all—his soul. And the depressed and despairing "victim" of chapter 3 who longed only for death is transformed into a man with a "careless rage for life."

What changed Job from the blessedly submissive man in 1:21 and 2:10 to the raging accuser of God in the dialogues? When did he first think his suffering was *punishment* for wrongdoing? He got it from his friends who would have reminded him that his experience was very like what Deuteronomy 28 outlined for transgressors. And it is this most painful of all experiences—his God has been taken from him—that is worked out in the exchanges. Assured by his friends that God has exposed his wickedness he insists there was nothing there to be exposed. Satan said his wickedness lay hidden behind good deeds that only existed because of good wages and that poverty and ill health would expose the wickedness. His friends said his wickedness lay hidden until God's punishment revealed it. From different angles both Satan and Job's friends accuse him of evil hidden beneath a robe of outward piety. Job screamed there was nothing there to be revealed! Instead of having the comfort of knowing that God was pleased with his heartfelt devotion he is now led to believe that God thought him a wicked transgressor. *They were stealing his soul!* And what added to his pain was that the God he has loved and served so well knew he was genuine and refused to vindicate him. No wonder he raged. No wonder he called his friends miserable comforters and false witnesses on God's behalf. He was the only one in the universe who maintained his integrity. And this was the man Satan said had everything but integrity!

10

THE CRY OF WHY

"You have taken from me my closest friends
and have made me repulsive to them....
I have suffered your terrors and am in despair."

Psalm 88:8,15

"Job opened his mouth and cursed the day of his birth . . . 'May the day of my birth perish, and the night it was said, 'A boy is born!' . . . Why did I not perish at birth, and die as I came from the womb? . . . Why is light given to those in misery, and life to the bitter in soul, to those who long for death . . . who search for it more than for hidden treasure . . .?' " Ouch! Whatever else this chapter does it shows Job is no unfeeling piece of granite. Whatever else it does it underlines the incredible nature of his blessing God in the face of such calamity. Feeling like this he still praised God?

Scholars like Habel have opened our eyes to the depth of Job's pain here. Some among us have been so pained that we felt like saying, "Stop the world. I want to get off." Job is so frenzied here he curses the world. His is the speech of "uncreation" and parallels the creation record of Genesis 1 (see the details in the commentaries). Because he is in such agony he wants the world to end; he's bitterly disappointed in creation and he wants God to join him in that disappointment (3:4). Because of his agony and fear the creation that he recently rejoiced in should now be cursed and shut down.

Then he follows with a series of agonized questions, "Why?" (11-23). His questions all make sense. In his state why wouldn't he ask them? And who is wise enough to answer them? As we stand before people who are beside themselves with grief and pouring out their questions we're reminded that our ignorance and silence half makes their case for them. "It's all pointless, isn't it?" Is that how Job felt? Since no one could give him the answers, did he think he had justified his emotional drive for uncreation? Perhaps so, but later God will speak to him about the creation he has just cursed and he'll tell Job that he is pleased with what he created. God will pour out his own cataract of questions that can't be answered and Job will know that the absence of answers doesn't make a case. See chapters 38-41 for God's response to Job.

Isn't it amazing how quickly the world can become hell? Do you think Job could have imagined himself saying such things when he lived in the sunshine? Even as he spoke them did his eyes not open wide at the self-revelation? Did he not wonder to himself, "Am I really saying such things?" They must have come as a shock to his friends but how would they have sounded to the Job himself who lived in the sunshine or the one who survived the storm? Some years ago a friend of mine made an absolutely dreadful tape that maligned the name of one of her loved ones. She told me with almost awe in her voice, "I could hardly believe that it was me who had said those things."

Life in a tidy, pleasant and consistent world doesn't prepare us very well for chaos and bedlam. Shattered people or those in deep depression say things they'd never dream possible and they learn things about themselves they can't possibly believe until the pressure is on. "Deny you? Never!" said Peter. "They might but I never will." Then a cock crows.

But of course once the passions have been inflamed there's no time for thought. Once the spirit has been crushed there's no capacity for hopeful visions. Once anger is in control the only thought is, "How hurtful can I make these words?" Joseph Parker of London confessed he never had a moment's doubt in his life until his wife died and for a while he thought like an atheist. Luther confessed that sometimes he believed and sometimes he didn't. It's easy, I suppose, for the calm types to be shocked at the vehemence and irreligion that comes spilling out of the mouths of those among us who are crushed.

I'm not speaking about people who never had time for God even when he was filling their lives with riches ("the Most High . . . is kind to the ungrateful and the wicked"—Luke 6:35.) I'm not thinking of those who ate and drank at his table but used his name for nothing but coarse and contemptible speech. When trouble comes to them it isn't surprising that they whine and complain that God isn't fit to be believed in. I've no wish to be rude but we expected no better of them. But when those who've known God from childhood and were richly blessed by him pour out language that's neither prayer nor praise we're shocked and often disappointed. It's for us to recognize the speech for what it is but if we're enjoying life in the sunshine we need to be gentle in our judgments.

Chapter three has been called the most depressing chapter in the Bible. It's true there aren't many like it and as a sustained piece not even Jeremiah's dirge or Psalm 88 matches it. A number of writers remind us that in the book of Psalms the "why?" sound is more prominent than "Hallelujah." Whatever else their function, these chapters and laments remind us that there is something out of whack in the world. Everything isn't all right! There *is* something to grieve about, something we *shouldn't* be reconciled to, something we shouldn't settle for.

Even the later harsh and unjustifiable speech of Job serves the same purpose as the honest lament of Scripture. It stresses the devoted man or woman's discontent with the way things are. There should be more to life than oppression, successful and entrenched evil, lifelong disease and victorious injustice. We don't need to settle for less and if we're refusing to settle, we're even doing God a service. It serves his purposes for us to remind humanity that the world is not now as God would and will have it.

Some of us, and there may be many more than I tend to think, would be willing to put up with anything. Too unsure of ourselves and maybe even too unsure of God to speak our minds. Too easily intimidated, too easily silenced. Like poor Linus.

> Linus is watching TV when Lucy walks by and turns it off saying, "Might as well turn this off. There's no one watching it."
>
> Linus' hair stands up on end and with a look of disbelief he looks into the dead TV screen and yells,
>
> **"No one watching it?"**
>
> He gets up and follows her, dragging his blanket, **"Waddya mean, no one? I'm someone!"**
>
> Lucy ignores him and strides out of the house with Linus shouting after her, **"You come back here and turn on the TV! If anyone is a someone, I am!!"**
>
> But she's long gone even though he's still yelling, **"I DEMAND that you come back here! Do you HEAR me?**

I'm a real someone!!!"

Now he's distraught, beginning to lose confidence and so less stridently he says, "**I demand that you come back here and turn on this TV!**"

Then he stands silent. Finally he sits down, wraps himself in his blanket, sticks his thumb in his mouth and with a beaten look says, "It was a lousy program anyway."

Linus' initial protests were right and he went after Lucy the way Job was going after God, the way many of the psalmists went after him. The good news is that God is not like Lucy. Linus finally settled for less than the best because he knew he was getting nowhere with Lucy. Her attitude killed hope and expectation.

Part of the reason deeply devoted men and women complain about the state of the world is because their God has led them to believe there's more. They wouldn't speak so plainly or complain so loudly if God wasn't the God they think he is. But it is *God* who gave them the words of lament, it is *God* who led (and leads) them to expect more. He enables them to see the world not only for what it is but also for what it could and should be. So the laments, the depressing chapters, and even the vile speech, bear witness to a planet in rebellion, a planet under judgment and out of tune, but on its way to full harmony.

But can't God wipe all this pain and torment out with just an exercise of his will? The Creator of the universe who has shown his unfathomable love for us in Jesus Christ has the (mechanical) power to do what he wishes; but maybe there's more involved than we know.

A little magic from God and we'd have an entirely different universe, but would it be the universe *he* wants? Would it be the universe *we* in our better moments would want? Would people be morally transformed or robots, would they choose to live in love with each other or be policed by God every second of their lives? Would it be the universe God is in the process of making this one into, in which dwells heartfelt righteousness? Why, in the meantime, must things continue as they are? I think we'll only get a fully satisfying answer to the "Why?" when we are able to see the completed picture. We can't make much sense of only a little fragment of an entire manuscript, but if we were to see the whole story the little fragment would make perfect sense. Until the entire manuscript appears, the fragment will continue to generate unanswered and unanswerable questions. But the fragment will testify to the existence of the complete story.

No one in his right mind would suggest that God like some divine hit man simply targets millions of babies and afflicts them with terrible diseases just to have another "teaching tool"! But it's true just the same that the presence among us of sick and helpless babies, retarded children and the defenseless aged points believers to a larger picture. And in the story of Job, the very existence of the ash heap with a disfigured and raging little man shaking his fist against heaven reminds us that something of galactic significance was taking place beyond the stars.

No one in his right mind would suggest that God like some divine hit man simply targets millions of babies and afflicts them with terrible diseases just to have another "teaching tool"! But it's true just the same that the presence among us of sick and helpless babies, retarded children and the defenseless aged points believers to a larger picture. And in the story of Job, the very existence of the ash heap with a disfigured and raging little man shaking his fist against heaven reminds us that something of galactic significance was taking place beyond the stars.

11

ELIPHAZ, AND WHAT DO YOU KNOW?

"The Tree of Knowledge is not the Tree of Life."

F.W. Robertson

Beware of friends called Eliphaz! The brilliant Scottish scholar, George Adam Smith thought, "The speeches of Job's friends ought to be studied by every man who proposes to make the guidance and consolation of his fellow-men the duty of his life. For these speeches are, every one of them, lessons in how and how not to discharge that delicate and responsible office . . . In particular, we have much to learn from the approach of Eliphaz the Temanite to his afflicted friend." I know he's right but Eliphaz made life hard for Job. He added darkness to the shadow Job was living in.

Being an Edomite would have recommended Eliphaz as an advisor since Edomites were known for their wisdom. In Jeremiah 49:7 we hear, "Concerning Edom: This is what the LORD Almighty says: 'Is there no longer wisdom in Teman? Has counsel perished from the prudent? Has their wisdom decayed?'" Since Eliphaz speaks first to Job it's likely that he's the leading figure among the three friends and when he speaks he begins gently, not wishing to offend (4:2) and he acknowledges Job to be a wise man also (4:3-4). But the situation is so painful to watch that he can't keep quiet any longer (4:2b).

The Temanite like his friends (like Jesus and Paul), believed in retribution, believed what you sow you reap, so in straightforward fashion he was sure Job was paying the price for some serious waywardness. He rehearsed a vision he had in the night, one that scared his hair to bolt upright. The truth of the vision was that humans are sinners and God punishes them for it. Some are worse than others and don't respond to God's chastisement and so they go down like a stone into the depths (4:12-21). Eliphaz doesn't think Job is one of the impenitent but he does think he is suffering because of some grave wandering. All that was required was for Job to repent, turn back to God and he would get all his material blessings back and die in old age (5:8,17-18,24-27).

Eliphaz was wise but wisdom isn't always warm and friendship doesn't make us infallible. Wisdom for all its courtesy and politeness is tempted to make everything a matter of "explanation." Things are often too cut and dried when wisdom is the chief element in the picture and what seems characteristic of wise men is that they lay no foundations. They simply "feel beneath them the great commonplaces" (G.A. Smith). It's hard even for God to break into the world of the wise to teach them new things. They have it all worked out; don't you see? The great commonplaces, the grand generalizations, the well-known truths—the established wisdom was once-for-all experienced, grasped, and memorized—what else is there to know? So when Eliphaz rehearses his frightening dream/vision we aren't surprised that it only reaffirms what he and his kind already knew. And when faced with a distracted sufferer like Job he explains all within the parameters of his inherited creed.

It's grand to be able to call on tradition and point people to the well-trodden paths. Chesterton was right, we should respect tradition. Democracy says a man's opinion is worth hearing even if he works for you and tradition says a man's opinion is worth hearing even if he is your father. Still, like all fine things, tradition needs to be watched carefully or it becomes a shrine at which we worship or a tyrant to whom we bow (which turns out to be the same thing). Paul in 1 Corinthians 1:18-25 makes it clear that human wisdom (even when it's God-given) can get in the way of God showing himself. If the sovereign Lord wants to do a new thing (like becoming human and dying on a cross to reveal himself) it isn't for human wisdom to forbid him. But that's just it, human wisdom does often forbid him. The narrative in chapters 1 and 2 show us a God who is willing to show himself in a new way—in a way traditional wisdom couldn't have come up with—so it really isn't surprising that everyone, Job included, flounders around trying to figure things out.

Wisdom is a fine thing but it leaves the wise open to pride in the wrong thing, pride in the wrong person. Jeremiah has a word to the wise ones in 9:23-24, "Let not the wise man boast of his wisdom . . . but let him who boasts boast about this: that he under-

stands and knows me, that I am the LORD, who exercises kindness, justice and righteousness on earth, for in these I delight. . . ."

The way Job defied the usual sage advice or seemed to claim an
extra measure of wisdom for himself rattled his friends and ruffled
their pride and it shows. In 15:7-10 Eliphaz is extremely irritated
with Job and says, "Are you the first man ever born? Were you
brought forth before the hills? Do you listen in on God's council?
Do you limit wisdom to yourself? What do you know that we do
not know? What insights do you have that we do not have? The
gray-haired and the aged are on our side, men even older than your
father." But it must be very difficult indeed to come across people
who resist the power of your wisdom—especially when you're
known for it—and strike out in their own direction. Wisdom *and*
patience don't always dwell in abundance in the same person. It
appears Eliphaz came up a bit short in the endurance area. *Beware
of a wise man that struts as he walks and is always looking at his watch.*

Wisdom is a fine thing but sometimes it can be as cold as a
northwest wind. I think it's the "logic" element in it all. There's no
doubt at all that Eliphaz really cared for Job but it's astonishing
how people can love their families and friends greatly and still be
brutal and cold in their treatment of people in general. Take
Eliphaz for example. Speaking of the wicked he says, "The righteous see their ruin and rejoice; the innocent mock them. . . ."
(22:19). His criteria for a good man include the good man's capacity to laugh at his enemy's downfall. And why not? Shouldn't we
rejoice when God punishes the wicked? It makes sense, but maybe
"making sense" isn't all it's cracked up to be. Jeering at an enemy
was an approach Job rejected in 31:29 when he says (implicitly)
that he hadn't "rejoiced at my enemy's misfortune or gloated over
the trouble that came to him. . . ." There was a warmth about the
passionate Job that Eliphaz seemed to lack. *Beware of a wise man that
doesn't need to light a fire in the winter.*

Wisdom is to be esteemed but it might be easy for a wise man to
overestimate the amount of it he has. I don't doubt Eliphaz had
earned his place among the wise but how wise can you be when you
say to Job, "What do you know that we do not know?" (15:9). Here
is Eliphaz the wise—healthy, wealthy and wise—talking to a man
who has just recently lost his entire family, his poor wife is driven to
distraction, all his wealth is completely gone and the status that goes
with it, his body is terribly disfigured and ulcerated, kids follow him

around jeering and drunks make up songs about him, his teeth have fallen out, he can't sleep and when he dozes off he's driven to wide-eyed wakefulness by terrifying nightmares. To top it all off, he feels a profound alienation from God—the one who matters most in all his life. And the wise man peevishly asks this desperate human being, "What do you know that we do not know?"

I would dismiss all that as hopelessly ancient except that the other day I met a pain-filled man who was hurt as a child and has been fighting evil drives ever since. He has been fighting against booze addiction since youth, lives in bitter self-hatred, already feels the sentence of doom, and has strong opinions he doesn't keep to himself. We had a sharp exchange about God and life and I was on the verge of asking him, "What do you know that we do not know?" and I thought of Eliphaz. *Beware of a wise man whose study door is overgrown with cobwebs and who carries cotton balls and a blindfold wherever he goes.*

Wisdom is to be sought and God gives it generously to the single-minded (James 1:5) but it's amazing how easily it can degenerate into a doctrine or system of "Success and how to achieve it." As soon as wisdom is severed from its root in and service to God, as soon as it becomes something that one cashes in on to bring about "success under the sun," as soon as it is secularized so that anyone can implement it, it has been corrupted and corrupts its exponents. It appears that Solomon used the wisdom God gave him to "succeed," and how well he succeeded! ("The half has not been told," said the queen of Sheba.) But in the process he lost his "effective" soul and wandered, godless "in all his glory" from the shrine of one god to another pursuing further kingdom success.

Then we have those who are too wise to bow to idols but use the wisdom to construct a system for business success. Books are written that can be read with profit (and without surrendering a single conviction) by atheists, agnostics and the irreligious. Biblical wisdom is narrowed down to a system of stratagems, tactics and skills that will result in one's business flourishing. Those who pay attention will be able to handle their employees better, production will increase, problem resolution will be easier and tension will be minimized if not eliminated. All very useful, no doubt, but equally fruitful if practiced by a moral reprobate or a righteous person. *Beware of a wise man that is invited to lecture on wisdom at "secular" venues.*

12

KEEPING MEN ON THEIR FEET

"I will speak of your statutes before kings
and will not be put to shame.... Oh, how I love thy law!
I meditate on it all day long."
Psalm 119:46,97

In a speech at the Royal Academy Banquet about the origin of literature Rudyard Kipling told of a man who did something marvelous but when he tried to tell it to his companions he wasn't able to put it into words. But there was someone who had seen the deed, someone who had nothing in him but the gift of words and he rehearsed the deed and the listeners discovered that the words were alive and "walked up and down in their hearts." Such is the power of words. Those of us who have provoked people to think words are cheap have a lot to be ashamed of but the poem which begins, "I'd rather see a sermon than hear one any day" is at best a half-truth that's in crying need of balance. Especially since the poem is a verbal sermon made up of *words!*

Friendly Eliphaz said to Job (4:3-4 NRSV), "See, you have instructed many; you have strengthened the weak hands; your words have supported those who were stumbling, and you have made firm the feeble knees." Moffatt vividly renders verse 4, "Your words have kept men on their feet." In this text Eliphaz is encouraging Job, so when he tells him to practice what he preaches now that Job's trouble has come, he isn't despising words—he wants Job to take them more seriously. He's lifting words up rather than bringing them down. The words in a great message are never cheap even when the speaker has cheapened himself so it's nonsense, and a crime against people in general, to despise or speak dismissively of speech.

It's almost humorous (but not quite!) to hear ministers make light of Bible study and earnest teaching by quoting James who is critical of those who merely talk and refuse to do. They seem oblivious to the fact that they're quoting words and that James is not exalting deeds above words; he's critical of those who pay no attention to the words! I'm speaking the truth when I tell you I've heard more criticism of "too much time" spent in the study of the Scriptures come from ministers of the Word than any one else. They are so anxious to be involved in the "practical" matters, they say, such as feeding the hungry, counseling the hurting, being involved in the community concerns and other "speechless" endeavors. Bless me, how can you argue with such involvement? Who'd want to criticize it? I suppose James, 1 John and Matthew 25 would come in at this point.

I'm sure we'd all want to be known as the kind of people the needy could call even late in the night about an emergency of a graver or lesser kind. It's right that we should be known as kind people, warm and helpful and anyone who has earned a reputation as a cold, unapproachable type should to some degree be ashamed of himself. That all makes sense to me but it's no excuse for one who professes to be a minister of the Word (especially one who is salaried in that capacity) to be ignorant of that Word. It's no excuse for an ignorant minister who prides himself on how little he knows and how little prayerful time he spends worshiping God by trying to think and trace out God's way with the world via the Scriptures. Such a minister should be ashamed of himself. It's the ill-conceived snobbery that is so distressing.

I want to protest the smugness of those ministers of the Word who pride themselves as *doers* and who leave people untaught, whose handling of the Word is a disgrace, whose prayerful study of God's word is at an absolute minimum, whose "ministering of the Word" is an endless regurgitation of the same worn-out clichés. I want to protest their refusal to take heed to their ministry which leads them to drone on and on unprepared and caring little that they are unprepared. No wonder people in general feel that getting into the Word is like licking carpet and just as fulfilling.

J.H. Jowett trenchantly remarks: "Without the discipline of hard study, preaching becomes raving. Without the wisdom that comes from sustained reflection, it becomes banal. And without abrasive encounter with science and scholarship, it becomes irrelevant. . . . If the study is a lounge, the pulpit is an impertinence."[viii]

It isn't news to say that there's a fast-growing and widespread illiteracy in the area of Bible. Observers from many disciplines are saying the same thing. In light of their calling, first and foremost, and in light of the growing ignorance, it's hardly-excusable nonsense to hear ministers of the Word use words to despise time spent alone in obedient, prayerful study. And in some ways, it's even worse, when as a substitute for rich involvement in the Scriptures, ministers shovel out secular pop-psychology (at a time when the most trenchant criticism of psychology is coming from accomplished professionals), interpersonal relationship counseling and opinions on current affairs or domestic and foreign policy. As if their failure to be faithful to the calling they profess weren't enough, they have to enter fields in which they are dabblers at best (they've read a few books) and utterly, transparently incompetent at worst.

A wordy man with no compassion or generosity is a disgrace. A compassionate and generous man with no message from God is sub-Christian. A teacher who is an impenitent gossip or immoral is contemptible and an upright teacher who, in speech or practice, is dismissive of his calling defies God. "There was a time," said Charles Campbell, "when the teaching and proclamation of the Word of God was seen as something marvelous in the world. It was seen as 'a weekly eschatological battle with Satan' but when preachers yawn about it, why would we think the church or the general public would think highly of it?"[ix]

I want to protest the hard and fast distinction between doing and studying or speaking. The very idea that meditating on and reading or speaking God's Word would *not* be regarded as *doing* the will of God would curl the toes of devoted doers of God's will. A slow, thoughtful reading of Psalm 1 is an education. (The Old Testament church didn't put Psalm 1 at the beginning for nothing.) A great doer of God's Word *said*, "Now I commit you to God and to the word of his grace, which can build you up and give you an inheritance among all those who are sanctified" (Acts 20:32). Of a great *doer* of God's will (see Job 29–31) it was *said*, "Your words have kept men on their feet."

It might be that we can't change sufferers' circumstances but maybe we can change *them* by speaking truth in love and enable them to either change their circumstances or live radiantly within them. Maybe wise and faith-filled words will keep some poor struggler on her feet. So fill yourself with the story, listen to God with earnestness and with as much desire as is in you to please him, and when the occasion presents itself you may find that words are more important than a simple "practical" response.

We should embrace people, feed them, spend social time with them, listen sympathetically to them, pay their bills when that's appropriate, paint their houses, mend their fences, baby-sit their children, mow their yards and any other lovely thing that will express our genuine concern for them but in God's name and for their eternal welfare we've got to teach them the living Word of God! There was a time when Jesus looked at his people and was moved with compassion because he saw them as sheep without a shepherd and he healed their sick (Matthew 14:14). We would expect no less of Jesus! When Mark 6:34 records the incident he says, "He had compassion on them, because they were like sheep without a shepherd. So he began teaching them many things." We would expect no less of Jesus! He saw them shepherdless "so" he taught them many things. Because he was ceaselessly teaching people the gospel of the kingdom of God the Master became known simply as "The Teacher" (Mark 14:14).

We've seen someone who had gone down into gloom and depression lifted by well-chosen, truthful, well-timed words, haven't we? Haven't we seen a woman dry her eyes and have her poor troubled heart comforted by warm, caring words? Haven't we seen a nation lifted out of dismay and paralysis by a proclamation of galvanizing truth? And didn't we read that Jonathan *talked* David out of despair by encouraging him in his God (1 Samuel 16 23:)? "Fan into flame the gift of God, which is in you," (2 Timothy 1:6) Paul told a young minister of the Word. "Do not neglect your gift. . . . Be diligent in these matters; give yourself wholly to them" he tells him in 1 Timothy 4:14,15. It is to both life and teaching that ministers are called (1 Timothy 4:16). Studying and proclaiming the word of God to the up-building and saving of peoples' lives is honorable work at which ministers are to be seen while they handle that word aright (2 Timothy 2:15).

13

WILL YOU JUST LISTEN TO ME?

"Father, I confess there is freer access to the
throne of grace than there is to my desk."
Elspeth Campbell Murphy

The approach of psychologist and guru Carl Rogers went well for a while if for no other reason than that many people felt, "At last, someone's listening to me!" That wasn't Job's experience; he felt he was having a conversation with friends who simply wouldn't hear him. He says in 21:2-3, "Listen carefully to my words; let this be the consolation you give me. Bear with me while I speak, and after I have spoken mock on." People in the shadows need people who will listen.

Poor Job (and poor friends)—his friends were well into their hewing and cutting job. They were pouring out words, thinking they were doing Job a favor. "This is the truth, the pure word of God," we can hear them saying. "We're offering you not only good advice but the consolations of God and you dismiss them." Eliphaz in 15:11 asks him, "Are God's consolations not enough for you, words spoken gently to you?" You only have to read how they were gutting him to see it wasn't only Job they were deaf to, they were deaf to themselves! Righteous people can get into a nice rhythm; pious words can flow easily and pleasingly. The pleasing rhythm gives them an added sense of truth. Scriptures come effortlessly to the tongue; truths from here, there and yonder join the stream, and before we know it we have a torrent of mighty truth tearing down all before it—including the sinner we came to save. "Words spoken gently to you," we tell them. What a spellbinding sight it is to see a righteous man or woman in full pursuit after a transgressor. No warrior in a Scythian horde or in the army of Ghengis Khan was ever so keen in coming to grips with an enemy.

Eliphaz self-righteously offers what he calls the consolations of God and Job sarcastically says as consolation he'd settle for their giving him a good listening to before they started mocking. "Will you just listen for once?" And somewhere a bullied wife, a frustrated husband, an accused child or a distraught parent is saying, "Will you just listen for once?" And the other stops talking, finishes off the sentence so someone else can talk. God help us, we think that's listening.

My wife, Ethel, has a very complex medical condition that includes paraplegia and associated re-routings. We were going to visit our grandchildren in America, a trip that physically wipes her out and generates all sorts of fears en route. The airline assured us that everything was taken care of but after about fifteen event-filled hours in transit we were relieved and ready to carry her on for our last plane ride. We were horrified to discover her seat was to be in the middle of a block of seats and mine in a different row. By this time I'd seen her badly transferred from wheelchair and back, almost dropped, jolted and frightened, spoken to abrasively, bumped against aisle seats and more. This was "too much" and I said so to the official at the door to the plane. At least if they weren't on the aisle we needed seats beside each other because things had to be tended to during the flights. He kept interrupting me, telling me there was nothing he could do, the plane was overbooked, I should have checked my seat assignment before I got to this point, and the like. The more he talked the angrier I became. I tried telling him again the physical situation and he again was shaking his head while I spoke—there was nothing he could do about it. It wasn't that I now expected him to reassign the seats—I . . . just . . . wanted . . . to . . . be . . . heard. I wanted him to feel my situation by understanding it. Yes, yes, maybe I wanted to see if I could get him to make some adjustment but I know I wanted to be heard!

God forgive me for all the times I've sinned in this way and hurt the hearts of those who really needed to be heard. In fairness, we're asking for a real gift when we ask people to listen to us. And if we've given people reason to be angry with us that makes it even harder. Because "listening" is more than saying nothing while someone else is talking. To listen is to enter into the part of the world they're living in and wrestling with. It's wanting to understand not only what these people are facing but what they are facing it with. Maybe they aren't wanting to be excused, maybe they don't expect that, can't expect it, have no right to expect it. Maybe they're just wanting to be heard and if they get that they'll soldier on!

Elspeth Campbell Murphy taught first graders for many years and thought that they taught her more than she taught them. In a lovely little book she wrote in 1979 she recorded the kind of prayers she prayed depending on the circumstances and needs. One of them was a prayer for help in listening to the children who were always so eager to talk. She confessed it was easier to get to God's throne than her desk and asked God for "a heart that understands the importance of a new pair of shoes or a lost pencil." She felt like a cheat because she rejoiced in the privilege of knowing that the Lord of the universe listened to her and she had a hard time listening to the children. It is a needed and lovely prayer that she concludes with, "and Father, thanks for listening." It's clear that listening is an art and a precious gift practiced best by wise friends.

In fairness, we're asking for a real gift when we ask people to listen to us. And if we've given people reason to be angry with us that makes it even harder. Because "listening" is more than saying nothing while someone else is talking. To listen is to enter into the part of the world they're living in and wrestling with. It's wanting to understand not only what these people are facing but what they are facing it with. Maybe they aren't wanting to be excused, maybe they don't expect that, can't expect it, have no right to expect it. Maybe they're just wanting to be heard and if they get that they'll soldier on!

14

WORDS AS WEAPONS

"If anyone is never at fault in what
he says, he is a perfect man...."

James 3:2

"Do not let any unwholesome talk
come out of your mouths...."

Ephesians 4:29

In the book of Revelation John describes the Dragon as a ceaseless accuser of the followers of the Lamb. We're left to wonder precisely what it is he accuses them of night and day before God. Since he's a liar, no doubt there are lies in all his prattling but since the followers of the Lamb are sinners there's probably truth in his slanders also. In any case, the earth beast that is the enemy of God's people is described this way (Revelation 13:11), "He had two horns like a lamb, but he spoke like a dragon." There it is, the innocent look but a dragonish voice. Harmless and gentle in appearance but demonic and destructive in speech.

There came a time when the distraught Job cried (19:2 NRSV), "How long will you torment me, and break me in pieces with words?" With words! "Sticks and stones may break my bones but words will never hurt me"? Of course it's true, and yet, is there anything more painful than a deep, barbed verbal thrust? Scalding, burning, agonizing words, "You dirty little—." "Hey, yeah you, stupid, come over here!" "Ah, shut your mouth! You're always whimpering about something." That's the straightforward, barbarian kind of stuff, from the stupidly ignorant and callous types.

Alexander Pope tells us there's another kind, more sophisticated but equally destructive, and he should know since he was a leading practitioner of verbal dismantling. He had a good grasp of the psychology of it all and could easily recognize the kind of people who:

Damn with faint praise, assent with civil leer,
And without sneering, teach the rest to sneer;
Willing to wound, and yet afraid to strike,
Just hint a fault, hesitate dislike;
Alike reserv'd to blame, or to commend,
A tim'rous foe, and a suspicious friend.

How easily words fall from our righteous lips. Armed with the rightness of our cause we carefully choose words that smart and embarrass, words that exacerbate guilt, words that humiliate, maim and isolate—yes, and isolate! How expert we can be. How like a skilled surgeon, wielding our verbal scalpels to wide-awake but helpless subjects before us—not an anesthesiologist in sight. A shallow but painful incision here, another there. Well placed for maximum effect. Wise and knowing, deliberate and calm, carefully thought through so no effort is wasted. The exhilarating experience of choosing just the right phrase that shows our not-so-nimble-tongued opponent is out of his league at best, or stupid at worst. And finally, when we've enjoyed as much of it as we can stand, the profound pleasure of going for the jugular or laying them open to the bone! Another masterful job completed. People already in the shadows are driven into deeper darkness.

Our *sister* will need a lot of nurturing and care before she can recover from the job we just did on her. Our *brother* will linger at the periphery of life (church and social) for some time before he gets over the "necessary" stripping job we did to him. And there's the wife we'd never dream of physically beating, but whose scars are scarcely less visible or the husband who writhes in silent and unseen agony because of the verbal acid dumped on him every so often. There are the parents and children who verbally rape each other and the rest of the time live in silence and resentment in the presence of one another.

How easily the words trip from the tongues of the self-assured. Thoughtless jibes and jokes, dismissed as nothing by the talker, but leaving the very sensitive a self-despising mass of exposed nerve endings. Pretending to take it all well, not wanting to appear easily offended, they smile nervously, wave (almost) good-naturedly and walk away in hidden agony, walk away before they burst into tears or begin to beg, "Please, no more. You can't know how deeply this is hurting me." *To speak violence is to do violence!*

The poet and playwright John Masefield gave us an unsettling look at all that in *The Tragedy of Nan*. Nan Hardwick's father was hanged for stealing and she was sent to her mother's brother to live. Her uncle's wife detested the girl and took every opportunity to make her life miserable. Ceaselessly critical, endlessly harping on her mistakes, real or imagined, and telling lies about her to everyone in sight. Even when it was proved that Nan's father had been innocent and the authorities owned up to it, Mrs. Pargetter still gouged her with verbal insults. Driven to distraction the girl finally exploded and yelled at her tormentor:

> You 'ad me in your power. And wot was good in me you sneered at. And wot was sweet in me you soured. And wot was bright in me you dulled. I was a fly in a spider's web. And the web came round me and round me, till it was a shroud, till there was no more joy in the world. Till my 'eart was bitter as that ink, and all choked.

In the war of words that went on in the book of Job, only God came out with dignity. It's easy to see, if we can patiently read through the dialogue between Job and his friends, how quickly everything got out of hand. The early, well-meant and kindly spoken words of Eliphaz are seized and shaken by Job the way a dog would shake a rat. One verbal onslaught led to another and before long they're hacking one another not only with truths they believed, but with scandalous things they didn't believe (compare 4:2-3,6; 5:8 with 22:5-9 and 6:15,27 with 19:21). And when that situation prevails there are lots of losers but only one winner.

"*Gooood* job, sir! I've rarely seen such a masterpiece of verbal dismantling. You're an obvious expert in this line of work. You must practice a lot or are you one of those 'naturals'? For a while I thought your opponents had you but you came back with brilliant responses, well barbed and nicely driven home. I especially liked the one where you told them, 'If you were to shut your mouths, now *that* would be wisdom'. I expect you noticed how they wilted at first before they got mad. I thought one of them was going to have a stroke. You're good, once you get going. You're as entreatable as a junkyard Rottweiler.

"Of course they handled themselves well too. Calling you a

'windbag,' accusing you of robbing your employees and callously mistreating widows and orphans were nice thrusts. But I thought their claim that you were a heretic was their most promising line.

"There's nothing I like better than a good slanging and slandering match. That really gives me a buzz. Truth is, I even get pleasure out of people putting one another down *in fun*. You know what I mean, you hear it all the time. It begins slowly but when they warm to it, they say things to each other that are less and less funny. It's good practice really. When they really want to hurt each other their tongues will be well oiled and at the ready.

"By the way, your name is . . .? Job! Of course, I knew that. It just slipped my mind. Pleased to meet you, Job. Who am I? I'm . . . ah . . . well, I suppose you could say I'm a troubadour of tales, some true, some part of the truth and some false (well, not 'false,' exactly, just not quite true, if you know what I mean). My name? Hmmm, I've lots of names. One of my favorites is 'Accuser'. Well, I need to go, my work's a real pleasure but it keeps me busy. Keep practicing and keep up the good work!"

And the shadows grow darker.

15

IN PRAISE OF GOOD FRIENDS

"'Stay' is a charming word in a friend's vocabulary."
Amos Bronson Alcott

Since sometimes they were all over their shell-shocked friend like junk-yard Dobermans, it isn't surprising that we often hear it said of them, "With friends like these, who needs enemies?" They tempt us to say that of them, but like so many generalizations, it passes by the fine things that were true of them. We make allowances for Job and we should make allowances for his good friends. God did. For all his rage against them, in the end Job recognized them for what they were—friends (42:10).

When they heard of the calamities that had befallen him they came to comfort him (2:11). I'm not interested in speculating if Job had other friends who didn't bother to make the trip—it's enough to say these three took the time to come to his aid. At different times and to different degrees, depending on the circumstances, friendship is costly and they were willing to pay the price. These men didn't come to abuse him, they came to console and offer their sympathetic support and we need to remember that they did this even while believing he had sinned. However difficult it is to find the balance between consoling a wrongdoer and acknowledging his wrong, a friend will wrestle with it so that compassion isn't blotted out in the work of convicting. God never loses his heart in his holiness and neither should we.

Many of us have been on the receiving end of a "loving barrage" which excused its merciless nature with the fine phrase, "I'm only speaking the truth, in love." Worse, many of us have been a part of such a hit-squad. But there isn't a reason in the world to believe that Job's friends came for any other reason than to share his pain and offer encouragement! In this they did well.

They sought to convict him of his sin. As it turns out, in this case the man was innocent even though the friends didn't think so. But however wrong they were, they acted (at least initially) in good faith and engaged in a genuine attempt to help. Where such a ministry is needed, this is an indispensable work of a true friend. What C.S.Lewis said of a father is true of a friend. It is utterly meaningless he tells us for a man to say, "I love my son but don't care how great a blackguard he is provided he has a good time." It is equally pointless for a friend to say he doesn't care if his friend is up to his neck in wickedness or being ravaged by sin. Friendship can't speak in this way any more than God can "drowsily wish you to be happy in your own way" (Lewis). If your friend is like God it will matter to him how you are morally and spiritually.

Lewis again. "To ask that God's love should be content with us as we are is to ask that God should cease to be God. . . . We cannot even wish, in our better moments, that He could reconcile Himself to our present impurities. . . ." To say our friend's love should be content to allow us to waste away in our sin is to ask our friend to cease to be our friend. When he will not do that, preferring to hurt us with truth if necessary, the words of the proverb are fitting: "Wounds from a friend can be trusted. . . ." (27:6). If our loved ones need to be convicted, it may be gutlessness that keeps us from confronting them. So in coming to Job to restore him to God they were friends indeed.

I need to offer two caveats. 1) If our friend is filled with shame and remorse over his wrongs, it is wholy empty-headedness that would lead us to pursue him "in order to convict" him. He's already convicted! His appearance and behavior make this clear. Only the one who doesn't acknowledge wrong (either out of ignorance or self-will) is a subject for the work of conviction. The weeping, distracted one needs another kind of help. 2) There may be an occasion when our friend is right on the edge of the abyss and while he won't acknowledge his guilt, it may still be a grave tactical mistake to pursue him to "own up." If he is so emotionally overwrought, your pursuit might mean permanent injury. Friends need to be wise. In such cases surely the wise thing to do is to nurture our friend while maintaining our integrity about the wrong we know him to be guilty of until he has the moral strength to make his own confession. The bottom line is not simply to convict him but to redeem him! Loving wisdom will learn how to combine both where it is possible.

They refused to skulk off because he became insulting. Ingratitude eats on us like acid. It's *so* hard to take. The friends came to help the man, they sat in sympathetic silence for a week and when they began to speak (in the person of Eliphaz) it's clear they meant well, their hearts went out to him. His response? An immediate withering blast against them, calling them hypocrites posing as friends. What an ungrateful wretch! Ingratitude not only galls us, it grieves us. The poet, Lord Byron, expresses it so well for us:

> So the struck eagle stretched upon the plain,
> No more through rolling clouds to soar again,
> Viewed his own feather on the fatal dart,
> That winged the shaft that quivered in his heart,
> Keen were his pangs, but keener far to feel.
> He nursed the pinion which impelled the steel;
> While the same plumage that had warmed his nest
> Drank the last lifedrop of his bleeding breast.

It's true that the three friends felt the bite and responded in kind but despite the bitter words they continued with the man even to the very end. Early on they might have excused themselves and walked off muttering something about people "biting the hand that feeds them." The temptation was real because they had come to help and all they got in return was abuse! Why should they put up with it? Why not go back home and let the ungrateful little wimp continue his descent into the dark? They didn't! God bless them!

In my own life (and I know I'm not alone in this) I have given friends good reason to walk away. Rudeness, ingratitude, wordless abuse, studied indifference, hyper-sensitivity and other things tempted them to wash their hands of me. They might have said, "There are insults enough in life without having to put up with them from someone you have served and given yourself to. Cut your losses and ease your pain." This isn't unreasonable advice, but neither Job's friends nor mine were eager to leave the needy one lying on the roadside.

They came to talk about God and Job's relationship to him. There's more to life than "God talk." There's a time and place for humor and silliness and my deep suspicion is that I'm in really short supply in that area of my life. I'm unbalanced as a person and while I might find it difficult to take it if I'm around a lot of harmless silliness for a sustained period, I'm in real need of people who know how to enjoy themselves without apology. But I can't shake the notion that society tilts too far to the side of entertainment and humor. I find it a source of great joy to be with those who, though much better balanced than I, still want to make God the center of everything. Job's friends were serious about God! They talked about God! They looked to God! They wanted Job to look to God! They thought when all was said and done that the supreme matter was God!

Yes, yes, they weren't all we in our better moments would want ourselves to be but they thought God mattered supremely. And it's true that they made grave mistakes but, bless me, I know people that, even if they were wrong in every statement they made, would affect nothing seriously because they never talk about anything worth talking about. You can only make major mistakes when you're involved in something that really matters.

Thomas Long in his commentary on Hebrews reminds us of something profoundly important. When church attendance was down, when bitterness and disappointment were gaining ground among believers and when suffering was taking its toll on their confidence and commitment the Hebrews writer didn't give them humor and platitudes. He gave them one of the most tightly argued theological books in the Bible. It was all God! He saw every problem as a theological one and offered God and his Word as the solution.

Must there not be little groups of angels gathered here and there in heaven, musing together and wondering with bewildered looks why it is that God's own people speak so little about him? And if there are, mustn't they be pleased to see life-loving, pleasure-taking men and women babbling on and on about God never dreaming that this is a strange thing to do? The day may come when we will look back in shame at our silence about God and in shame at our ignorance of the Scriptures. Then maybe we'll look around and see those strange beings we raised our eyebrows at, the ones who couldn't keep from talking about him and making him the center of everything. And we'll thank God for them as the instruments of our own salvation and our enrichment.

16

TO RAVE OR NOT TO RAVE?

"For [God] knows that even their rebellion is a
form of service which he can accept with joy, since
what he desires is the homage of free spirits."

E. L. Allen

Eliphaz in 4:17 uses the same words as Job here in 9:2 but they're not asking the same question. In 4:17 Eliphaz was comparing the moral glory of God with his sinful creature man. In 9:2 (NRSV) when Job asks, "How can a mortal be just before God?" he is not asking what kind of life a person needs to live before God to be pleasing to him. He's insisting that once God condemns you it doesn't make any difference that you're innocent, you're pronounced guilty and there's nothing you can do about it! You can't win a lawsuit against God Job is saying. How can you out-argue someone as mighty and as wise as God? Here he admits God's almightiness and omniscience but as far as Job is concerned, God's power doesn't honor him, it shames him because he uses it to abuse the innocent and oppress those who are defenseless before him. You'll remember that Job prided himself on his defense of the vulnerable and marginalized (see chapter 2, "They Scarcely Believed It").

Here's a question: Is it wrong to slander God? Here's another: Is it wrong to slander God even if you're suffering terribly? I don't think God is made of crystal. I don't think he will fracture if we rant and rave against him. Hasn't the world been doing that from the beginning and he's still around? Isn't that what we did while he hung, stretched out on a cross for all of us? He's not going anywhere and our abusive speech won't lower his self-esteem.

Nor do I think God is overly sensitive. I don't think he debates with himself whether he will sulk in silence with us forever if we snarl ungratefully at him. I don't think he is so engrossed in his own self-importance that he peevishly turns away from us when we don't give him the honor and reverence due him. I don't think he wants us to grovel at his feet every waking moment and I don't think he watches, always verging on bad temper, waiting to deliver a smashing blow from a huge fist to those of us who dare to look heavenward with a fierce protest.

I don't even think that God wants to stifle our snarls, protests or verbal pain with threats of reprisal. I know we have the record of some people under some circumstances being cut off in midstride (he buried a whole generation in the wilderness), but these are the exceptions that prove the rule: God is long-suffering, slow to wrath and filled with compassion.

I don't think God is unwilling or even slow to forgive. I don't think he keeps detailed records of how often we come to him with confession and prayer to find forgiveness. I don't think he measures pardon out on a gram-scale or has that "Are you here again?" look when he sees us approach, covered in our shame and looking for cleansing.

The question here isn't, "Will God forgive us if we scream and snarl unjust accusations at him?" The question is, "Is there anything that needs to be forgiven?" Let me be clear about what it is I'm opposing here. I'm not opposing Job's saying that God is responsible for his pain and loss because I agree with Job, I think God is responsible for his losses. What I'm addressing are his accusations against God of child abuse! I'm thinking about his insistence that God perverts justice, favors the wicked, abuses the innocent and defies anyone to do anything about it.

I believe Job was wrong to accuse God in such a scurrilous way as, for example, in 9:22-24 where he says, ". . . I say, 'He destroys both the blameless and the wicked.' When a scourge brings sudden death, he mocks the despair of the innocent. When a land falls into the hands of the wicked, he blindfolds its judges. If it is not he, then who is it?" When God finally speaks to Job out of the storm he rebukes him for his unbridled speech. God didn't come to destroy Job because he had spoken that way, he came to bless him but in the course of blessing him he rebukes him. Here's what God said to him in 40:8, "Would you discredit my justice? Would you condemn me to justify yourself?" God admired and loved the man and that's why he wagered on his faithfulness in chapters 1 and 2 against the satanic cynicism. But he rebuked him when he sinned!

When Jeremiah accused God of being an unfaithful deceiver (15:18) God rebukes him for it by saying (15:19), "If you repent, I will restore you that you may serve me; if you utter worthy, not worthless, words, you will be my spokesman."

I think it's wrong to say that radical pain or loss justifies just about anything we feel like saying to God. At times I get the feeling there's no such thing as blasphemy. I get the impression there's nothing you *can't* say to God if you really feel he has let you down. Let me repeat: I think God is more than willing, he's eager to forgive us, but I think there is something to forgive. As I write this I'm very aware that this all seems to run counter to what we read in the book of Job but I don't think it does.

I don't think it is either right or healthy to teach people that it's all right for them to use God as a punching bag if they're in real pain. I think this is wrong for all kinds of reasons; not the least of which is this: The God we would insult and damn is the one who would not spare even his own Son but abandoned him for us all (Matthew 27:46; Romans 8:32).

Is this what we're supposed to say to the bereaved and suffering? "Yes, yes, I understand, you feel betrayed by God and you're hurting terribly. I just want you to know that it's all right to insult God and accuse him of heartless injustice under these circumstances." "Yes, I know you've been redeemed by the boundless love God showed to you in the sacrifice of his own Son, but right now you're enduring awful hurt so it's okay to insult and malign him for not keeping you from this pain." This is what fellow-believers are to say to one another? Do we really think this is true?

Let me make another thing clear. Anyone who approaches a serious sufferer to rebuke for reckless speech is an idiot! Can you imagine rebuking a newly released survivor of the Nazi death camps for his savage denunciations of God as faithless? In the words of Samuel Johnson, "Such excess of stupidity, sir, is not in nature." You aren't born that stupid; you have to learn it. Not only would it be bad pedagogy it would be insufferably self-righteous. Even to raise the issue would surely be the act of an insensitive clod.

There's an excuse for devastated people when they use slanderous speech, but it's hardly excusable for ministers of the God and Father of the Lord Jesus to call it righteous. My own observation has been that when the *utter* agony of his/her experience has finally passed, the believing sufferer brands his/her slanderous speech as inexcusable and then wonders about a minister who holds their views while his life is filled with blessing. It doesn't help to say that it's good therapy to unload our wicked accusations, or that God is capable and willing to put up with them. It's astonishing what people claim is "good therapy."

God is capable and willing to bear *all* of our wickedness, done even in less troubled times, but that's just the point, he has to *bear* it. And it may ease our emotional pressure to accuse him of child abuse but whether this is good for us in the long run is another question. Even if we are to grant it is good "interim therapy" that doesn't justify it or make it something we should nurture in people.

It's a crass blunder to believe that the only way, or even the best way, we can help people who are so tortured that they speak unjustly against God is to align ourselves with their speech, to join with them against God! To encourage people to pour out the pain of their poor hearts to a God who is eager to listen is one thing. To encourage them to spit out their venom as though it were the certain proof of authentic faith is something else.

Whatever else the book of Job's there for, it isn't there to encourage us to slander God and think it is right! But what if the speaker truly believes God is immoral and sadistic? Well, then, he will speak the distortions he has embraced won't he? But should we say that ignorance that leads to slander doesn't arise from sin? Is it not true that our distortions are part of the darkness that exists because of human rebellion?

Somewhere down the line God's self-revelation in the biblical witness, and in Jesus Christ in particular, should grant him some immunity from savage slander from *his own people!* And all the more since we have greater light than Job.

Let me repeat. What I'm opposing here is the kind of talk that urges people to believe that God's character is truly a matter of doubt. I'm opposed to our teaching people it's all right to speak slanderous things of God if you are suffering. I'm opposed to our saying that the sometimes-scurrilous speech of Job is what we're supposed to aim for in our Christian maturation as part of an "authentic" faith.

If we think a person is in too much pain and that pointing to the long history of the love and kindness of God toward us isn't the appropriate thing to do at that moment, sympathetic silence might be the best thing. What is surely a mistake is for us to join with the victim in his accusing and slandering of God. Heaven forbid!

Francois Mauriac who had known the pain of the war years himself, listened to the heartbreaking story of Elie Wiesel who was then a young journalist. Wiesel was tormented by the pain of loss and by God's watching but doing nothing about the Nazis. Mauriac couldn't bring himself to tell the weeping young man that the utter injustice of the Holocaust experience which had destroyed Wiesel's faith was, in the Golgotha experience, what created his own faith. He couldn't bring himself to say that, so he simply embraced Wiesel and wept sore with him. That was a Christlike response!

However tender we are, however hurt we are by the sufferer's hurt, however much sympathy or empathy wells up within us (and we should apologize for none of this!) and however we choose to involve ourselves with the sufferer's pain—whatever we feel or do, we should never side with the sufferer (or sinner) *against God! There is something sinister going on when we offer comfort to someone at God's expense. Resist the temptation to do it!*

Having said all that, what E.L. Allen said is true and begs to be heard.

> If conscience finds the course of things unjust, whence did conscience arise? For conscience is part of the world it condemns. Strange world, indeed, to make provision thus for an adverse judgment to be passed upon itself!
>
> This protest also must be from God. So man realizes with Awe what is happening. Like Job, he is appealing from God as men have misunderstood him to God as in his heart of hearts he knows him to be. So that, in the last analysis, his opposition to God is the work of God in him. God wants men to challenge him and bring all things under the judgment of conscience, even if in so doing they pit themselves against him. For he knows that even their rebellion is a form of service he can accept with joy, since what he desires is the homage of free spirits, of persons who have it in them to rebel against him but who instead surrender themselves to him in utter trust and loyalty. Such surrender is only possible to those who have dared to God himself to account.[10]

I have no wish to take issue with any of this nor ask for further clarification on some things because centrally it is so true and rich that we need to rejoice in it. "Such surrender" is only possible to those who remain with God even while they rave because they have pain enough to warrant raving.

17

FRIENDLY FIRE

"If a blind man leads a blind man, both will fall into a pit."

Matthew 15:14

"Brother, let me take the speck out of your eye...."

Luke 6:42

Life on the ash heap is hard enough without our friends adding to the pressure and the pain but it's an injustice to Job's friends to deny that they were anything other than true friends. The only thing we know about them is what the narrator tells us and he told us in plain terms that they were his friends, that they came to comfort him, and that, when they saw his terrible state, they were smitten with sympathetic speechlessness.

Even in the heat of his pain and anger Job appeals to them as his friends. Even as he rebukes them in 6:14 he calls them his friends. In a heartbreaking appeal he says in 19:21 (NRSV), "Have pity on me, have pity on me, O you my friends, for the hand of God has touched me!" Even at this late stage he still regards them as friends (of course!) and wants them to stand by him while God is putting him to grief. And when he emerges from the crucible we're told in 42:10 that he prays for "his friends." Through it all, despite all the bitter things they said about each other, these men are friends to the end.

But they made mistakes. Sincerity doesn't alter the fact that sometimes we kill those we mean to help. They die, as more than a few soldiers have, from friendly fire. Love must grow in wisdom and wisdom must be made humble and kind by love.

The friends should have taken his word for it that he was innocent of any crime which would warrant 'punishment' of the kind they thought they were witnessing. I don't share the view that they along with Job held a *hard core* retributive justice doctrine. They didn't *have* to interpret his awful state as God's punishment on his terrible wrongs. There were other possibilities. (Joseph's career in Genesis shows that suffering can be vicarious.)

Of course a friend in his shame can lie to you so Job's claim of innocence may have been a lie. *Because* upright people are ashamed of their dark deeds they want to hide them. I'm not saying that's always healthy nor am I saying that lying about such things is right. (Nor am I saying that "blabbing about our sin" is confession *nor* that it's healthy!) I'm saying that the desire to cover up is understandable! The reason pious people do their evil deeds in the dark is perfectly plain—*they're too ashamed to do them out in the light!* Would you expect them to? That decadents and degenerates parade and boast of their wickedness is no surprise to anyone.

I once heard a man whose life had been one of characteristic faithfulness to God but who had dug a bad hole for himself—I heard him being criticized in words like, "Can you imagine him sneaking around doing that?" When I asked if we expected such a one to do it openly, there was no comment. *Of course* we sneak around! Whatever else is screwed up within us there remains a healthy degree of shame that won't permit us to flaunt our sin; that won't even permit us to admit it too quickly. When we lie about our involvement in the shameful, it's a lie, of course; but it isn't always hypocrisy! Maybe more often than not the sense of shame, *which is a mark of genuine piety*, is what motivates the lie. We can hardly bear to have others see us as we have been. Impious degenerates don't act that way. It's too easy for the stony-hearted (whose own sin isn't seen) to say that evasiveness and even lies exist for no other reason than the worst form of self-protection. There is some form of self-protection involved but it need not be that the transgressor simply wants to retain the right to further crimes without detection.

So I know Job *could* have lied to them but they had no factual evidence whatever for doubt! It was Job's glorious life against an arguable interpretation! But for some, the risk is too great. They don't want their own garments to be stained by association nor do they want to be thought of as "soft on sin." So, in self-defense, they sever their ties with the accused. For a strong devoted friend the risk of identification with a sinner is nothing.

While they didn't need to agree with everything Job said, they should have made allowance for the terrible suffering he was undergoing.

If you believe a friend has been trapped in sin, it is no crime to try to extricate him. If you have reason to think your friend is being sucked into or has been entrapped in sin, not only is it no crime to go to his aid, it would be a crime *not* to. We should not apologize for an attempt to help in such situations. If it turns out we are wrong, that our fears are unfounded, no one, not anyone(!) will be more pleased to be wrong than the devoted friend.

But bearing in mind that they were dealing with a man right on the edge of the abyss, pain-filled, bereaved, diseased, isolated by the community, mocked by those he had helped and counseled; a man in his agony, is slowly beginning to see God as a demon-hunter of his life, they should have proceeded with more caution and kindness. He begged them to recognize that his words were rash because his multi-faceted pain was unbearable. It doesn't appear they remembered that for very long. These are tough *righteous* men and there aren't many rocks, hidden in the earth or on the end of a cutting machine, harder than a righteous man on a righteous mission.

They trapped God behind a specific doctrinal stress and made him a prisoner of their theology. All these men (Job included) believed in divine retribution but they had no good reason for making that doctrine into God's master and lord. *Of course* they were right in teaching God blesses righteousness and punishes evil! Anyone who comes away from the book of Job thinking he has been "cured" of that doctrine will be made sick again by the rest of the biblical corpus. The doctrine is taught everywhere in the Bible.

And, yes, it needs to be carefully structured and nuanced but what's strange about that? Just say, "God answers prayer!" and you'll have generated more questions than you can answer in a lifetime. Because it's a complex truth doesn't mean it isn't truth. The doctrine of retribution isn't the *only* truth and it *is* a complex truth. To take one truth as if it were all truth is the way to eventual blindness. To take one aspect of a complex truth and stress it to the virtual exclusion of all other aspects of that truth is the way to tyranny and bigotry.

That in part is where I think the friends went wrong. They weren't wrong to say God punishes sin and blesses righteousness, they were wrong to make that the only truth that counted, the only truth that could be operating here. And that *interpretive* move meant they joined their voices to Satan's against a man who was completely innocent of any fault that warranted his great suffering. This made them opponents of God! They made God a prisoner of proverbs and maxims and it resulted in needless added suffering for an already suffering fellow-human who was heroically doing battle for them against cynical forces. Proverbs embody wisdom and that wisdom is from God but it doesn't exhaust God, it isn't absolute like God. When God is here, a greater than Wisdom and all her maxims is here.

They equated his (alleged) sin with his character rather than with some out-of-character transgressions. At first Eliphaz (and so the other friends) saw Job as a man of character who had committed some wrongs, but when he refused to admit this and began to pour out his verbal agony on them and God, they changed their view. They began to accuse him of wickedness that rose from a corrupt character (see especially 15:5). A character, they said, that had been established many years earlier (see 22:4-11 where Eliphaz claims wickedness was always true of Job).

This is a grievous wrong against a friend! What made it worse is they had no certain knowledge of *any* wrongs. But even if they had (and Job had never been slow to admit sin when he was guilty—31:33-34), that didn't give them the right to invent and speculate that there were others. It didn't give them the right to conclude he had a godless core for a heart. They trashed the whole man's life on the basis of some (alleged) particular sins.

Considering how passionately we hate others doing that with us, considering how unfair it is, how arrogant it is, how merciless it is, you'd wonder that we do it at all. This is one of the reasons we should think on things of "good report." We have no right to dismiss the testimony of all the good that people do, think, feel and aspire to. We need to let those aspects of the man/woman have their say and bear their witness because they will help deliver us from a merciless trashing of a whole person on the basis of some specific wrongs.

Wrongs are wrongs and shouldn't be whitewashed but there's something very wicked about burying an entire person beneath the debris of specific wrongs. Shame on Job's friends. Shame on us! For sensitive transgressors who are caught in their own net, there is already powerful self-despising. When the upright insist that the specific wrongs are proof of a corrupt self, something more is added and a tragedy is in the making.

All along Job has insisted on his innocence (and because he is strong he will continue to do it), but he does experience the horror of self-doubt at the character level. His pain, the cutting words of his friends and God's hand in it all takes its toll every now and then and he loses his inner way. The Jerusalem Bible gets it right, I think, in 9:20-21:

> Though I think myself right, his mouth may condemn me; though I count myself innocent, it may declare me a hypocrite. But am I innocent after all? Not even I know that, and, as for my life, I find it hateful.

I confess that criticism from friends is an awful torment for me and if the criticism is because of my transgression, it sears beyond words. But if my friends were to take my specific sins and make them my life and construe them as a full definition and meaning of me as a person, I might just shrivel up and literally die quickly.

To see ugliness in ourselves, to want to run away and hide from it, fearing that the ugliness is the ultimate reality, is terror. To have friends come and confirm our deepest suspicion—that's our worst nightmare. "I don't know myself" (9:21, Habel). To know I sin is one thing. To be persuaded I don't love God or care to please him is paralysis of the soul. If I come to believe that with seriousness the next thing is, "as for my life, I find it hateful."

Friends must be careful that they don't push their friends to the edge of the abyss with their merciless appraisals. Friends must be careful that their friends are not already on the edge of the abyss and need only some brutal confrontation to trigger their leap into spiritual oblivion. Tragic things have happened that led those who helped provoke them to put their hands over their mouths in shocked silence and mutter,

"I didn't realize...."

But they made mistakes. Sincerity doesn't alter the fact that sometimes we kill those we mean to help. They die, as more than a few soldiers have, from friendly fire. Love must grow in wisdom and wisdom must be made humble and kind by love.

18

WHAT IS MAN?

"Astronomically speaking man isn't worth noticing."
Elmer Barnes

"Astronomically speaking man is the astronomer."
John Doe

I notice when I'm in pain or experiencing loss the whole world revolves around me. If it's a really severe case I have little or no time to think about anyone else, little interest in thinking about larger questions or theological explanations. But now and then I think I do my best thinking when I'm feeling the burden of such things. I suspect that is true for most of us, don't you?

I'm sure Job experienced that. Almost always he has himself in mind, his own pain, his own bewilderment, his own frustration, his own weariness and near-despair. When he speaks it's usually "me" and "I" that dominate his thoughts and speech and when the sense of loss is especially acute he forgets completely the years of blessing he enjoyed. In that respect, acute pain or loss tends to make us ungrateful and shorten our memories. Still, every now and then Job rises above his own personal agony and loss and makes contact with humanity in general. In chapter 7 he sees humanity from at least two angles. He sees people as sufferers and sinners and he feels hurt for them on both counts.

Job now sees himself as part of a humanity in which there is too much sorrow, too much pain, too much of everything that narrows and steals the life out of life. In 7:1-2 he groans, "Does not man have hard service on earth? Are not his days like those of a hired man? Like a slave longing for the evening shadows. . .?" (See also 14:1-4.) Of course he knew about this before and had been deeply involved in doing lovely things to ease the burdens of fellow-humans; but it's a different kind of knowing now. When good and generous people are involved in easing burdens they see them more clearly than those of us who don't see fit to involve ourselves, but that kind of work has its dangers too I suppose. When you're on the *helping* end the burdens are real but when you're on the receiving end they're real in a different way. A surgeon has a different view of a malignant tumor than the patient with cancer. It wouldn't surprise me if the patient would be happy to swap perspectives with the doctor. The 1991 movie *The Doctor* with William Hurt is a good illustration of the point.

In any case, now knowing at a personal level how they feel, Job enters into their pain and not surprisingly he does it at God's expense since he's angry with God for his own personal reasons. But now that he thinks about it, the Creator and Provider doesn't do such a great job for humanity at large. While he has no sympathy whatever for the violent and the oppressors, on the whole, he's sure humanity has a tough existence. This is an expensive insight; one he would never have had as he now has it because of his trouble. It's still costly for anyone who truly wants to enter into an understanding of the human condition because it takes a bit more than reading Hugo, Dickens or George Gissing. Those of us whose lives run smoothly are able to see what's going on in the world but talk like this, talk like Job's, is hard for us to enter into emotionally. You don't have to be an Einstein to know that it's hard for people who are chronically ill or ceaselessly oppressed to keep a civil tongue in their heads. If it isn't God they're mad at it's the society and authorities around them that do nothing about the injustice that's rampant. Or if they don't have enough energy to be angry they don't have enough to pay any attention to a God who doesn't seem to care about them. Do you find that strange?

But it isn't just the suffering and deprivation that guts Job and his fellow humans. There's the sin issue and the moral structure of the world. You know only too well that Job thinks God is unjust and that enrages him but he's also burning about the claustrophobic nature of the moral governance of the world. Human beings are feeble and shaped to become sinners from the moment they are born. Because that's true, Job thinks God is too hard on them and he lashes out against him in 7:3-10, for why should a beaten human stay quiet? "The Lord of all Righteousness" won't give humans a break. "Am I the sea, or the monster of the deep that you put me under guard?" (7:12). Job screams. Is Job or any other feeble human a threat to world order or worth bothering about? It's all too absurd; this is a divine battleship with missiles fully loaded pursuing a beetle! Does God enjoy frightening him (and people like him) by punishing them for their sins? Does he give him and them life and use it as an instrument of torture? If so, Job would much prefer it if someone would put him out of his misery. "Mercy killing" would be no bad thing.

Then he parodies Psalm 8 with this, "What is man that you make so much of him, that you give him so much attention, that you examine him every morning and test him every moment?" (7:17-18). Sarcasm drips from every syllable. David in grateful but astonished praise in Psalm 8 wonders why God is so good to man, why he pays him so much attention, honoring him so. Job, offering no praise but still in astonishment wants to know why God is so cruel and why he makes such a big deal out of man's wrongs. "Will you never look away from me, or let me alone even for an instant? If I have sinned, what have I done to you, O watcher of men?" (7:19-20 and see 10:20).

Job and his friends all agree that God is infinitely above humanity and that would mean he must be so far above man that he can't be affected by human sin (see 7:20; 35:6; compare also 22:3). That makes sense, but only if it is isolated from other truths. With those truths in mind (that man is puny and lives a tough life and God is infinitely above humanity) Job is incensed that God makes a big deal of human failings. What does he expect? He punishes humans because they aren't God? For Job this makes God appear all the more malignant when he ceaselessly watches them every second. Moffatt renders 7:20, "If I sin, what harm is that to thee, O thou Spy upon mankind?" The bottom line is that Job thinks God is guilty of overkill in the extreme.

You must understand that Job isn't making a case on behalf of the cruel and brutal and malevolent or those who live slyly and unrepentantly on the misery of their fellows. He looks around the world with a new understanding, sympathy and fellow feeling for the rank and file. And to the Almighty, the always-in-the-right Lord, he would have protested, "And these you never take your probing eyes off of? These you come down on with the weight of a mountain? So what if they've sinned? What do you expect? They've been born into it and shaped by it, how then can they avoid it? You're away up there and they're way down here—why do you make such a big thing out of the sins of such puny creatures? What difference can it make to you? Why do you have to hurt them so? Why can't you just forgive them and go on (7:21)? Even if they are decent and fine and work hard to be good and to be free from sin they are still vile compared with you (9:29-31). But what's new about that? Not even the guardian angels are pure compared with you (see 4:18-19). *Must the world be a slaughterhouse or a slave camp because you are infinitely better than we are?"*

The truth that God is infinitely just mustn't be the only truth we tell. When only that truth is told the whole of creation becomes a courthouse, humanity becomes a mass of criminals and the only matter of importance becomes handing down sentences! And if God's chief concern is punishing sin, humans will become preoccupied with sin and punishment rather than life and joyful obedience. Gloom settles in because where there is only just punishment there is no warmth and where there is no warmth there is no relationship or affection.

Bad enough that our overriding view of God is that of a zealous Judge who worships the law, it's made worse by the truth that for us humans sin is inevitable. It isn't just "trouble" humans are bound to experience (14:1), they're bound to experience sin—how can they avoid it? By the time they're of the age to reflect on such matters they are already bent in favor of doing what is sinful. The world humans are born into subsequent to the revolt in Eden is precisely the kind that "manufactures" sinners. David is astounded by his crimes against Uriah and Bathsheba and says the only thing that can explain it is that from the very beginning he was shaped to sin (Psalm 51:5). (We don't have to believe in a poorly worked out Calvinism to know we are pervasively corrupt and that our corruption began long before we made our first conscious choice to sin.) Humans are vulnerable to viruses and bacteria but no more so than they are to the sin "virus." If God punishes us for our sin and our sin is inevitable—what a rip off! All right, so God is "just" and does no evil. But is his "justice" the legalistic kind? Is it cold and clinical, the kind that can freeze salt water? Maybe we can't convict him of injustice but can we convict him of being stingy and ungenerous?

These are important issues raised in the book of Job. Even Christians under pressure can be heard saying, "All right, God cannot be unjust but is he guilty of overkill? All right, he can't be guilty of overkill but does he lack generosity and warmth? Yes, it's true that sinners choose to sin but are they biased in favor of sin by forces too powerful for them long before they actually choose to sin? If that's true, are these not extenuating circumstances that should be taken into account by God when he's judging sin?" Job thought so and so do I. Job didn't have as big a picture as we do and in light of the coming of Jesus Christ we have reason to believe that God is generous and not coldly "just." We have reason to believe that sin can never look as ugly and devastating to us as it does in God's eyes. But while God is implacably hostile to sin and will never view it as a trivial matter we have reason to believe his love for humanity can't be fathomed. No one sees our vulnerability and weakness more clearly than God and no one seeks our blessing as relentlessly as God.

So what is Man? Whatever else humanity is,
it is the apple of God's eye.

Job didn't have as big a picture as we do and in light of the coming of Jesus Christ we have reason to believe that God is generous and not coldly "just." We have reason to believe that sin can never look as ugly and devastating to us as it does in God's eyes. But while God is implacably hostile to sin and will never view it as a trivial matter we have reason to believe his love for humanity can't be fathomed. No one sees our vulnerability and weakness more clearly than God and no one seeks our blessing as relentlessly as God.

19

JOB AND ZOPHAR: A WAY OF SEEING THINGS

"Snatch from His hand the balance and the rod,
Re-judge His justice, be the god of God."
Alexander Pope

Devine said Zophar "is just the man to take a hammer and hit a nail on the head, but the last person to do a delicate piece of moral surgery—probe a sensitive conscience, remove the source of irritation, and tenderly bind up the wound." (I know a man like that!) He's offended by Job's torrent of words and dismisses him as "this talker" (11:2). Job's life and reputation are reduced to a "torrent of words" because he is now (viewed as) a transgressor. Later Zophar's pride is hurt and he, hardly able to wait to speak, says, "I hear a rebuke that dishonors me, and my understanding inspires me to reply. . . ." (20:3). We've seen it so often and have ourselves been guilty of it so often one might think we'd be done with it by now but we aren't. If someone insults us *God* becomes a terminator from another world! I mean, if we're insulted not only do we call God in to rebuke the offender, the God we call in (via biblical texts) is harsh beyond measure. God won't apologize for carrying out justice (though he confesses to Ezekiel he has no pleasure in wrath that is terminal) but let one of his insulted spokesmen get going and you'd think God was made of nothing but devouring fire on the outside and cold, unfeeling marble on the inside.

Speaking out of his hurt pride and wanting to "stick it" to the sinner Job, Zophar spells out the fate of the wicked under God (20:5,14,15,18,21-22). "The mirth of the wicked is brief, the joy of the godless lasts but a moment . . . his food will turn sour in his stomach . . . he will spit out the riches he swallowed. . . .What he toiled for he must give back uneaten; he will not enjoy the profit from his trading . . . his prosperity will not endure. In the midst of his plenty, distress will overtake him; the full force of misery will come upon him." The trouble with this description is that it just isn't true! Though he insists he is speaking the sober truth that has been plain since the beginning of time (20:4) he is doing no such thing. His frustration with Job and his wounded pride have torn the bridle from his tongue and led him to say things that are simply not true. The fallacy of them can be seen "ever since man was placed on the earth" by anyone with a single eye and half a brain

But a soured or angry heart has a hard time seeing properly and an equally hard time bridling its speech. In its ugly way it takes hold of all the truths that support its agenda and ignores everything that would lower the temperature. Did he trespass against me? Here! Here are forty passages that deal with transgression and every one of them thrusts the wrongdoer down to a hot hell. It doesn't matter that the bulk of the texts are not parallel to the situation facing the angry one. This isn't the time to be fair much less merciful so if the verses *look* like they're useful pour them out. The sour heart is unwilling, because it is unable, to see things in the best light. Two people can look at the same thing and interpret them differently. Paul Scherer reminds us that when Ecclesiastes sees the sun rising and setting, rising and setting, rising and setting the teacher takes it as proof of the moral indifference of life. When Jesus sees it he says it proves his Father's faithful generosity in making the continuously rising sun to shine on the wicked and the good. Qoheleth would say, "See, it doesn't matter if you're evil or good the sun shines on you both." Jesus would say, "See, the sun shines on the evil and the good. Isn't my Father generous!" (Modern scholars with a deistic type approach should take note! Everyone knows that the creation "in and of itself" favors no one, but since there's no such thing as the creation "in and of itself" such talk is worse than irrelevant. The creation is totally under the control of the ever-working Father—compare John 5:17.)

Job's bitter response to Zophar's angry overstatements is equally off balance. Here's how he describes the fate of the wicked. "Why do the wicked live on, growing old and increasing in power? They see their children established around them, their offspring before their eyes. Their homes are safe and free from fear; the rod of God is not upon them. Their bulls never fail to breed; their cows calve and do not miscarry. . . .They spend their years in prosperity and go down to the grave in peace. . . . the evil man is spared from the day of calamity. . . . He is carried to the grave, and watch is kept over his tomb. The soil in the valley is sweet to him; all men follow after him, and a countless throng goes before him. So how can you console me with your nonsense?" (21:7-10,13,30-34a). Like Zophar he is sure that this is common knowledge (21:27-29), which is why he calls such talk nonsense. But Job isn't being realistic either. Of course there are many wicked who prosper and whose children are educated with the money extorted from the voiceless and defenseless but in his heart Job knows better than to say God doesn't judge the wicked. Though he says it, he knows better than to believe the wicked don't suffer—they certainly do. Obviously not all of them suffer in this life but he has seen what we have seen, people who are wicked who suffered greatly and for a long time before they died.

Our emotions carry us away. A psalmist filled with joyful trust in and praise for God says that though he is an old man he has never seen the child of a righteous person going hungry. This is the speech of a lover and not a clinical recorder of facts. He was an old man so he had seen his share of suffering and he had seen the righteous go hungry but he knows he has never seen God forsake his loved ones. His pleasure at the presence of the faithful God leads him to dismiss as nothing the occasions when God's people have gone through tough times. This is the reason love covers a multitude of sins in our loved ones, isn't it? And we, when we're angry with those who've sinned against us, have no time for passages on compassion and forgiveness. Smarting because of the hurt brought by our opponent we overstate our case and become false witnesses for God, leaving God saddled with a harshness that isn't in him. On the other end of the spectrum those of us who are having a very difficult time forget the good times we had and look at everyone else with an envy that blinds us to their troubles. We all know that the proverb "The way of the transgressor is hard" is based on enough experience to warrant the truth of the general saying. In his pain Job overstated his case. In his anger and pride Zophar overstated his case.

It's difficult to maintain modesty under pressure. Before we know it we're making claims about things way beyond our grasp and speaking for God in a way that God will not speak for himself. Zophar was saying what God *ought* to be doing to the wicked and

Job is saying God isn't doing what he ought to be doing. They looked out at the same world and saw different things. In each case it wasn't enough for things to be as they were, these men had to doctor the facts, emphasizing this, ignoring that and presenting a lopsided picture of God's reality. For one reason or another they were as discontent as we are with how God handles things so they acted, as we often act, in God's name without his permission. I wonder why we find it easier to take God's place on his throne than take his place on his knees (John 13)? The brilliant Alexander Pope in his *Essay on Man* (epistle 1, verse IV) brings our sinful tendency home with great power when he says:

> Go, wiser thou! And in thy scale of sense,
> Weigh thy opinion against Providence;
> Call imperfection what thou fanciest such,
> Say, here He gives too little, there too much:
> Destroy all creatures for thy sport or gust,
> Yet cry, If man's unhappy God's unjust. . . .
> Snatch from His hand the balance and the rod,
> Re-judge His justice, be the god of God.

20

SAUCE FOR THE GOOSE

"... in the same way you judge others, you will be judged,
and with the measure you use, it will be measured to you."
Matthew 7:2

Believing as I do that Job's friends didn't *need* to see him as a rebel against God, they should have given him the benefit of the doubt when he said he was innocent of any wrongdoing that would account for his terrible troubles. They were his friends, and apparently long-time friends. They came to comfort him and were so distressed by what had happened to him that they sat in silence for a week thinking that sympathetic silence was better under the circumstances than talk. And when later they begin to chew on him he says he's terribly disappointed in them because, "A despairing man should have the devotion of his friends, even though he forsakes the fear of the Almighty" (6:14). Of course, he isn't confessing that he has run away from God—he insists on his fidelity and expects his friends to believe him.

In 6:28-30 (REB) Job makes this heartfelt protest, "So now, I beg you, turn and look at me: am I likely to lie to your faces? Think again, let me have no more injustice; think again for my integrity is in question. Do I ever give voice to injustice? Have I not the sense to discern when my words are wild?" You can hear the vexation in him when in 16:1-5 he calls them miserable comforters and says it would be easy for him to gouge them if the roles were reversed, even though he wouldn't do that to them. If things looked bad against them, he would remain lovingly loyal.

In 19:1-6 he pleads with them again to believe him when he says he is innocent and then he poignantly says, "Have pity on me, have pity on me, O you my friends, for the hand of God has touched me! Why do you, like God, pursue me, never satisfied with my flesh?" (19:21-22 NRSV).

As you know, the soul-shaking thing for Job is that God himself appears to have proved faithless! The most immediate pain (though not the deepest) is that his own faithfulness has been denied and he is regarded as a monstrous sinner. *God is faithless and faithful Job is the one being gouged.* How can he ease his pain? Who can he tell his story to and find sympathy? He should have been able to appeal to his friends; but they ignored the years of integrity, the years of watching one another grow up in the Lord, the years of faithfulness and grace. They dismissed the memory of ten thousand lovely words they had heard him speak and a thousand kind deeds they'd seen him do. The friends chose to forget the tears they saw him weep over the plight of the poor, chose to forget the money he discreetly slipped to those fallen on hard times, chose to ignore his forgiving ways toward his critics and how he was saddened when his enemies lay dying. They chose to ignore the fact that Job was so filled with reverence and awe for God that it led him to worry even about his family's faith response (1:5). For such a one to rebel against God would take some believing!

His friends ignore his record and it strikes him as unutterably unfair of them. They took his life's history and trashed it! Okay, they had a doctrine of retribution but so had he! Their doctrine didn't *compel* them to take this view of their friend. There *were* other options, and they *should have* looked for other explanations! They knew that sometimes the innocent came to grief and they should have seen Job in that light.

That's how he would treat them, he said, if the roles were reversed (16:4-5). He would give them the benefit of the doubt; they would have his comfort! *It didn't seem to dawn on him that what they were doing to him he was doing to God!*

The way he rages against God, slandering him in the plainest fashion is breathtaking. You might be tempted to think Job had never known God's friendship and blessing. You'd be tempted to forget that God had a history, a life with Job, that should have allowed him the benefit of any doubt but, once Job got going about God, it was all daggers at close quarters. He rages at what his friends are doing to him and does the same to God.

Job to his friends: "Does my life with you down the years count for nothing?"

God to his friend: "Does my life with you down the years count for nothing?"

Job to his friends: "Won't you give me the benefit of the doubt?"

God to his friend: "Won't you give me the benefit of the doubt?"

Job to his friends: "You're faced with something you don't understand so you accuse me of all kinds of wickedness?"

God to his friend: "You're faced with something you don't understand so you accuse me of all kinds of wickedness?"

Job to his friends: "You don't have a sure answer so the choose the worst?"

God to his friend: "You don't have a sure answer so you choose the worst?"

Job to friends: "You admit there are difficulties but you judge at my expense even though my life up to this time, as you yourselves know, has been exemplary?"

God to his friend: "You admit there are difficulties but you judge at my expense even though my life up to this time, as you yourself know, has been exemplary?"

Job to friends: "Aren't friends supposed to remain loyal to one another even in tough times?"

God to his friend: "Aren't friends supposed to remain loyal to one another even in tough times?"

I don't want to understate Job's pain but I think he could have given God the benefit of the doubt. I can see that a man would scream in agonized protest and it makes sense to me that in his pain he wouldn't be especially interested in a theology lesson. But from our vantage point the goodness of God to Job all the years from birth to mature manhood shouldn't have been ignored. It might sound like I'm being glib but resist the temptation to think so because I only want to make the point that if we want to be given credit for our record (which is no bad thing!) we ought to extend the same privilege to God. Sauce that's good for the goose is good for the gander.

I confess to being a bit weary of hearing from ministers (rather than serious sufferers) that "authentic faith" just about *requires* us to malign God. It seems that in some circles a submissive heart that bears suffering graciously but without violent protest is some kind of offense. To stagger under a sudden and colossal loss and to go on gallantly with, "It is the LORD; let him do what seems good to him" (1 Samuel 3:18 NRSV) suggests fear rather than faith to a lot of writers these days. Some of us hurry by a submissive Job who blesses God in 1:21 and 2:10 so we can get to chapter three and onward where he begins to malign God. "Ah, now that's true faith!" we seem to say, "Prior to that it was Stoicism."

Some writing and preaching would make you think Franz Kafka, author of the terrifying *The Trial* wrote the book of Job and left out all the clues. I confess it ticks me off a little to read (as not long ago I did) a Christian scholar warmly recommending a book (calling it courageous and fine) that seriously accuses God of inexcusable child-abuse. The author who endured the Holocaust does not tick me off, there's something Joban about him, but I have no sympathy with the reviewer whose faith is centered on God's own Child. Are we truly to pretend that it's an open question? Let's see, the God and Father of our Lord Jesus Christ might *actually be* the ultimate child-abuser? We're supposed to suspend judgment on such a question if our faith is to be authentic? No! Say from morning till night that we haven't the *foggiest* notion how the existence of suffering and sin fit into the scheme of the Father of Jesus Christ but don't pretend you think God might *really* be an omnipotent child-abuser. If that's "authentic" faith—we ought to pass on it!

Let those who've been through purgatory and have now entered hell feel they have reason to suspend judgment about God's ultimate nature and purpose for humanity. From them we can understand it! But let's have none of this "authentic" twaddle from thrice-blessed men and women who preach and write to glorify Jesus Christ and bring hurting people to faith in his Father. Maybe God has earned the right to be given the credit we want given to ourselves.

I don't know if George Herbert would agree with what I've just written here or not but I agree with this poem he wrote saying he can't get to the bottom of (skill) God's ways or his own (*Justice 1*):

I cannot skill of these thy wayes.
Lord, thou didst make me, yet thou woundest me;
Lord, thou dost wound me, yet thou dost relieve me:
Lord, thou relievest me, yet I die by thee:
Lord, thou dost kill me, yet thou dost reprieve me.

But when I mark my life and praise,
Thy justice me most fitly payes:
For I do praise thee, yet I praise thee not:
My prayers mean thee, yet my prayers stray:
I would do well, yet sinne the hand hath got:
My soul doth love thee, yet it loves delay.
I cannot skill of these my wayes.

I don't want to understate Job's pain but I think he could have given God the benefit of the doubt. I can see that a man would scream in agonized protest and it makes sense to me that in his pain he wouldn't be especially interested in a theology lesson. But from our vantage point the goodness of God to Job all the years from birth to mature manhood shouldn't have been ignored. It might sound like I'm being glib but resist the temptation to think so because I only want to make the point that if we want to be given credit for our record (which is no bad thing!) we ought to extend the same privilege to God. Sauce that's good for the goose is good for the gander.

21

THOUGH HE SLAY ME

"My God, my God, why have you forsaken me? . . .
Father, into your hands I commit my spirit."
Matthew 27:46; Luke 23:46

The NIV renders 13:15, "Though he slay me, yet will I hope in him . . ." which is close to the KJV "Though he slay me yet will I trust in him." T.K. Cheyne, one of the first Anglican scholars to throw his weight behind the "higher critical" approach to Scripture, called the KJV rendering "an inspired mistranslation." Most other versions give an almost opposite rendering, suggesting that Job denies himself hope. The NRSV has, "See, he will kill me; I have no hope" but offers the KJV as an alternative in the footnote. Since the scholars debate it, the linguistically ignorant among us have nothing to offer. In the end, says Andersen (who favors the KJV) the matter will be determined by what the reader thinks of the context because the text is laced with various linguistic possibilities. (See the scholarly literature.)

Regarding context, my own opinion is that Job is experiencing conflicting feelings and so expresses himself ambiguously. Maybe that's why the synagogue has two different readings of the text. One is as the consonants sit and is called "as written" (*kethib*)—"He may well slay me; I have no hope." On this showing the words speak of despair or defiance or both but as it is "to be read" (*qere*) the words tell of a stubborn commitment to God—"Though He slay me, yet will I trust in Him."

Whatever else is true, it is characteristic of Job that he feels more than one thing at the same time, as we often do in difficult circumstances. In 14:7-12 he says that humans die and that's the end of them but then in vv. 13-17 he entertains the longing that he would die but that God would keep him safe in death and call him back to life and vindicate him. Then in vv. 18-22 that daring wish, if the word "hope" is too strong for what he feels, is driven from him and despair bubbles back to the surface.

Maybe something of that same ambiguity is felt here in 13:15-16. He wants to argue his case with this unfair God (13:3) because his friends are useless (13:1-6). But even though he thinks God is unfair he still feels in his bones that he (God) esteems truth (7-12). It's that kind of conflict he's feeling when he says he will make his case before God even though it is putting his life at risk (13-14). He says he thinks God will kill him (15a), which says he thinks his case is hopeless but even as he says that, it strikes him that maybe he won't! If Job insists on making his case before God, trusting himself to God, maybe that will be his salvation (16). No obviously ungodly person would be eager to meet God and plead innocence. The fact that Job is anxious to do just that might persuade God that his servant has been faithful. But even that assumes God can be trusted to be and do what is right. Remembering that the man who dares to think this is disfigured and devastated, it is an incredibly noble thought.

Though not textually connected, the Ninevites had the same feelings of ambivalence when they heard Jonah's strident message that Yahweh was against them and purposed to destroy them. The whole city repents at Jonah's message and the king says (3:8-9), "Let everyone call urgently on God. Let them give up their evil ways and their violence. Who knows? God may yet relent and with compassion turn from this fierce anger so that we will not perish." Who knows? Maybe God won't slay us. We will repent and if he slays us, he slays us!

This reading of the text might be paraphrased, "I think God will kill me so I've no reason to hope. Still, maybe the very fact that I'm eager to put my case will show that I'm innocent and God will be persuaded by it. I've been acting as though he is completely unfair but maybe that isn't true. Well, I'm going to trust myself to him and if he kills me, he kills me."

It's a matter of continuous amazement to me that people can still wrestle with and about God in the most horrifying situations. It's true of course that many people are in too much pain to think of anyone but himself or herself. That makes sense but it makes it more astonishing that men, women, girls and boys in the Nazi death camps and tens of thousands in the gulags devoted themselves to prayer, praise and theological discussion. Why didn't they simply turn their backs on God? Some survivors of those camps have told us that they no longer believe God exists because they'd rather believe he wasn't there than believe that the Omnipotent sat watching the unspeakable without moving; better not to exist than bear such shame against your name.

I don't mean to give the impression that those who maintained faith in those places of horror held their faith in quiet submission. The faith was real but the protest at the time was unceasing and savage. Believers like this who maintained faith under such brutality reminded God that he had made commitments too. Elie Wiesel was then a teenager and was part of a crowd that stood without food watching three victims hanging and dying. His rage against God made him feel stronger and nobler than God. These people who lived only to do God's will, speak his praise and study his Torah were getting what in return? This ceaseless humiliation, abuse and torture while the God they served watched in silence? It was too much, his faith demanded more than God had come up with, so as far as he was concerned it might as well have been God who was hanging there instead of the little boy. I don't find that strange. I find it breathtaking that in their millions they went to God through the gates of death with faith-inspired protests. (See a Wiesel quote below in chapter 23, "Out of the Whirlwind.")

Job for all his rage and fear and uncertainty has nowhere else to go, has nowhere else he wants to go but to God. It is *God* he wants to get it right with. God, not his friends, not the world, not society. If he can get it right with God the rest will be bearable, the rest will work itself out but he can't live with any kind of peace unless he gets it settled with God! He is less sure about God than people like Ezekiel, Habakkuk and many psalmists but he has still experienced enough of God in his life that he cannot convince himself that he should curse God and die. He will take his life in his hands (13:13-14) and take whatever God dishes out.

Though he slay me yet will I trust him!

Job for all his rage and fear and uncertainty has nowhere else to go, has nowhere else he wants to go but to God. It is God he wants to get it right with. God, not his friends, not the world, not society. If he can get it right with God the rest will be bearable, the rest will work itself out but he can't live with any kind of peace unless he gets it settled with God!

22

VIVERE ERGO HABES?

"They overcame him [the Dragon] by the blood of the Lamb
and by the word of their testimony; they did not love
their lives so much as to shrink from death."
Revelation 12:11

"Oh, that I were as in the months of old, as in the days when God watched over me; when his lamp shone over my head, and by his light I walked through darkness; when I was in my prime, when the friendship of God was upon my tent; when the Almighty was yet with me, when my children were around me. . . ." (29:2-5 RSV). Anyone who can't hear nostalgia here is listening too hard in other directions. In this defense of himself Job can't help saying he misses his divine friend and wishes things were different.

Dying isn't the real enemy. Living without God is the *real* enemy! It's clear that Job missed the blessings of God. How could he not when his bones were crumbling, his diseased skin was falling from him, pain wracked his body, his family was gone and his reputation was shot? It's equally clear that he missed his God, missed the friendship they knew. For Job, dying would have been a gift in many ways, death was over-rated (3:20-23) and that's how tens of millions in every generation view it who have to struggle every day to get enough to eat and who wretchedly watch their babies make a slow, drawn-out exit from the world. To Job it was *living* with God that was precious beyond words, death in general was a secondary issue.

Still, death meant something more sinister to those who lived in pre-Christ days. Even sickness had its sinister side because it was seen as the approach of death. Conceptions about life after death varied in ancient times and with different people, from the view that "there is no life after death" to "there may be life after death" to "there's life after death but it lacks the vitality that makes life, life." Speaking from a Christian standpoint, which is shaped by the Christ himself, to make biological life the supreme value is sub-Christian. This straight speech from Reinhold Niebuhr may be hard to swallow but the real question is, is it the truth?

> It is easy to be tempted to the illusion that the child of God will be accorded special protection from the capricious forces of the natural world or special immunity from the vindictive passions of angry men. Any such faith is bound to suffer disillusionment. Nor does it deserve moral respect. Stoic indifference toward the varying vicissitudes of mortal existence is preferable to lobbying, with whining entreaties, in the courts of the Almighty, hoping for special favors which are not granted to ordinary mortals or godless men. The ultimate security of a noble faith lies in the assurance that "all things work together for good," but not that all things are of themselves good, or that the faithful will escape vicissitudes which are of themselves evil rather than good.[11]

Sterner than Niebuhr was Tertullian who wrote a tract *On Idolatry* and in chapters 5, 8 and 12 he speaks to those artisans who said they had to continue making idols and decorating idol temples since they "had to live." Tertullian snaps back, *"Vivere ergo habes?"* He wants to know who told them they "had to live"? If they had made that decision without God, he bluntly tells them, why bother about God at all? He insisted there is only one "must" for the Christian and that is to remain faithful to the Lord and his Christ. And somewhere, years ago, I read a poem triggered by Tertullian's challenge. I can't now trace it but a piece of it went *something* like this:

> "A man must live!"
> We justify every sin to treason high,
> A little vote for a little gold,
> A whole senate bought and sold,
> With this self-evident reply, "A man must live!"
> But is it so?
> In what religion were you told "a man must live"?
> The time will come when a man must die!

Imagine for a battle cry,
On an army's banner carried high,
This coward's whine, this liar's lie,
"A man must live!"

When it's our time to die will we insist that God keep us alive or we'll level scurrilous accusations of heartlessness against him? While the overarching purposes of God remain incomplete, humans are "born unto trouble as the sparks fly upward" and nothing will change that. A religious faith that will not face the tough realities of life as we now know them, while God moves toward the completion of his loving purpose—that faith is a poor substitute for the one offered in the Scriptures.

Part of the reason I suppose that so many of us in the West live in anxiety is that we put too much value on comfortable living and painless, instant dying. Then again, how many of us want a prolonged and agonizing death (as Ignatius died)? The preacher Dinsdale Young never tired of telling his students that the last thing they could do for God in this world was to die for him. Gazing around at them as they sat transfixed he'd say, "See you do it well."

How can we whose whole existence and faith are created and shaped by someone who chose to give up his life for us, how can we whose faith and hope have been created and shaped by someone who would not spare his own Son but brought him to death for us—how could we, without qualification, say, "Well, after all, a man must live"?

Where would we be now if the Christ, before Pilate, lonely, spittle-covered, bruised, friendless and in some key areas still struggling for understanding—where would we be if he had talked his way out of the judgment hall, avoiding the cross and finding his own life? What if he had been heard to murmur to himself as he walked to freedom, "Well, a man must live!"?

IV
LIFE AFTER THE STORM

*How can we whose whole existence and faith
are created and shaped by someone who
chose to give up his life for us, how can we
whose faith and hope have been created
and shaped by someone who would not
spare his own Son but brought him to
death for us—how could we, without
qualification, say, "Well, after all,
a man must live"?*

23

OUT OF THE WHIRLWIND

"Oh, the depth of the riches of the wisdom and knowledge
of God! How unsearchable his judgments, and his paths
beyond tracing out! Who has known the mind of the Lord?
Or who has been his counselor?"

Romans 11:33-34

We've seen it in the movies again and again. Big John Wayne listens to the bad guy shoot off his mouth until he has had more than enough. Then, without warning he's all over his enemy like a bad case of measles. How will God react when he finally steps in to respond to the bitter tirade of Job? He doesn't come to destroy but to bless, even while he rebukes, and *he comes talking!*

I can hardly imagine the fright Job must have experienced when he heard the voice of God, but at least God was finally talking to him. Utter silence is such a painful experience, isn't it? Even between human lovers who have had a very serious difference that (sullen) silence is traumatic and painful. After a prolonged, fear-filled silence even stern words are a blessing; even heated argument is blessed change. Words—even words meant to hurt— say the speaker thinks the relationship is worth bothering about. The voice that frightened Job must also have lifted him in some way but the words certainly didn't explain anything.

Nobody is sure just how God's speech in chapters 38–41 functions. It isn't hard to make general suggestions and give some arguments to support these suggestions, but that's just the problem. It's easy to give *all* kinds of interpretive schemes some support but there is no view that jumps right out of the text and demands that we accept it. With some justification Tsevat has called God's speech "education by overwhelming."

Some things are obvious enough even if the specifics of the

overall argument are unclear. Job is shown his ignorance (what do you know?), his powerlessness (what can you accomplish?), his lack of wisdom (what do you understand?) and his lack of consistency (if that bothers you, why don't these other things bother you?). This is *a man* who wishes to sit in judgment on God and it *appears* that God is saying to him, "What makes you think you have the right to challenge my righteous governing of the world? If you don't have the qualifications to be God, why do you express your opinions as though you were God?"

Among other things, Job lacked modesty. This is a man who railed against God and demanded that he come down and face Job like a man. This is a man who insists that the sovereign Lord should be accountable to him, should come at his beck and call, and should be under Job's control.

He had poured out his questions and if God would just show himself, he had said, he would put a lot more questions to him. Unanswerable questions, questions that would surely prove God to be unjust. Then God finally speaks, out of a storm. Job had been pouring out his questions in desperation but with some insolence and self-assurance. Now that God has confronted him he says (40:4-5), "I am unworthy—how can I reply to you? I put my hand over my mouth. I spoke once, but I have no answer—twice, but I will say no more." The Voice drives home Job's past insolent questioning (40:7 NRSV), "I will question you, and you declare to me." The first question he puts to Job goes right home to the first and most needful thing of the moment (40:8), "Would you discredit my justice? Would you condemn me to justify yourself?

God meant Job no harm! But he didn't come in a storm for nothing. He didn't come down in some quiet hour, sit by the man with his arm around his shoulders and gently say, "Well, do you feel better now that you've got that off your chest?" I'm not suggesting he was foaming at the mouth in rage against Job! God admired this man, was pleased with the character that led him to stand up against injustice even when he thought it was God who was unjust. God loved the man and *because* he loved him he rebuked him for his insolence!

Then he conducted Job on a tour of the physical world. A world the man didn't create, a world he knows nothing about and a world over which he has no control. From the heights to the depths, on earth and in the skies, from the foundations of the continents to distant galaxies God whisks Job in a cosmic survey. Enough to take his breath away, enough to remind him how small he is (40:4). Enough to create some modesty in him (42:3). Who is wise enough to construct such a universe? Who is wise and powerful enough to keep it working? Who controls the elements and can make a desert flourish (38:25-27) or end a drought by bringing rain from heaven (38:34-38)?

And all around the human is a world filled with creatures beyond his control. Wild goats who thrive in independence, beyond human control (39:1-4), wild donkeys who sneer at towns and ignore human commands (5-8), wild oxen that will pull no human plough or bring in no human harvest (9-12), silly ostriches that laugh and scoff at shrewd human hunters (13-18), wild horses that fear no human and respond to their own inner drives (19-25) and wild birds that scornfully live without human permission (26-30).

Then there are the wild humans who practice wickedness and live off the life's blood of the defenseless and voiceless. What about these? Can Job act to control these, to put them in their place, to bring them down to the grave (40:10-14)? Let him try his hand at that and God might take him seriously as a contender for God's office.

We might sense better the effect all this would have on Job if we imagine God waiting after each question for Job to answer, "No!" Can you do this? No. Have you seen this? No. Can you control this? No. Do you understand this? No. Were you there when this? No. Have you searched out? No. Are you wise enough to? No. Can you explain this? No.

And does this poor little human, who can neither understand nor tame anything, think he can understand or domesticate the sovereign God? He, who can't get a donkey to pay attention to him, does he think he can call God to heel? One that the comical ostrich laughs at, will he take himself so seriously that he will order God to make an appearance and take his medicine from someone like Job?

I mentioned elsewhere that in C.S. Lewis's *The Horse & His Boy*, the human hero finally meets up with the lion Aslan (the Christ-figure in this series). He has been through some very tough times and he complains to the lion about it all. There had been so many dangers and among them, perhaps the most terrifying, were the lions, the lions that roared in the night, the lions that followed them everywhere, frightening them and sometimes wounding them. Aslan tells him there was only one lion but Shasta knows better than that.

"Of course there was more than one lion, why . . ." Aslan repeats there was only one lion and that it was "swift of foot." When the boy asks him how he knows that, Aslan soberly informs him that *he* was that lion. The amazed Shasta finally asks him, "Who *are* you?"

"Myself," said the Voice, very deep and low so that the earth shook: and again, "Myself," loud and clear and gay: and then the third time, "Myself," whispered so softly you could hardly hear it, and yet it seemed to come from all around you as if the leaves rustled with it.

Lewis wanted to tell us of the incomparable majesty of the Lord Christ. Something like that is happening here in God's speech to Job. Shasta's response to the Voice is revealing too. "Shasta was no longer afraid that the Voice belonged to something that would eat him, nor that it was the voice of a ghost. But a new and different sort of trembling came over him. Yet he felt glad too." The fact that God has manifested himself to Job and Job hasn't died would have created both a trembling and a gladness. Confronted with his own puniness and the overwhelming presence of the Sovereign, no wonder Job doesn't want to talk (40:3-5; 42:1-6). It's true he had stressed his weakness in many of his speeches but sometimes he was doing it to elicit pity rather than to truly acknowledge the weakness. It's also true that though he spoke of his human puniness, he felt bigger than God, better than God, stronger than God. For example, he insists that God has wronged him and that it would be lies if he said differently. It was *God* who lacked integrity and so in 27:5 (NRSV) he says, "Far be it from me to say you are right; until I die I will not put away my integrity from me."

We find this in Elie Wiesel's very moving account of a night in the Nazi death camp. It was New Year's night and ten thousand Jewish men gathered together to pray and praise God before eating the food they were starving for. As the leader choked out the words to bless the Eternal and as ten thousand voices responded, the teenage Wiesel felt his rebellion and told himself that man was greater than a God who would let this cruel obscenity go on. "I felt very strong. I was the accuser, God the accused. My eyes were open and I was alone—terribly alone in a world without God and without man. Without love or mercy. I had ceased to be anything but ashes, yet I felt myself to be stronger than the Almighty, to whom my life had been tied for so long. I stood amid that praying congregation, observing like a stranger."[xii]

And so, Job (whose situation was not nearly as difficult as Wiesel's), while he *spoke* of his weakness, his ignorance and lack of wisdom, only finally *felt* it, when he found himself in the presence of God. And maybe that's all that's needed sometimes. In light of God's past history with Job and ourselves, in light of his past blessing and goodness, maybe it's enough for us to remember that we're ignorant and powerless and learn to be modest. And if we're modest maybe we won't clamor for explanations and, despite our pain and questions, we'll trust in God. Christians need to remember that since Christ has come they have more reason to trust God than people like Job do.

Still, there is some suffering that's so demonic in its fury or callousness so diabolical in its shrewdness that words—even words of Scripture—stick in our throats. Say the biblical words in a church building or a synagogue, say them around the coffin of a much-lamented friend who lived a long life and died in peace and they seem fitting. Speak them in Cambodia, Dachau, Siberia, Haiti and numberless other places and they sound cheap, to be dismissed with anger and impatience. This makes God's words to Job all the more galling. Let me repeat, there's no word of apology, no word of explanation, no revealing of what went on behind the scenes, no sitting down with him on the ash heap with an arm around the crazed man, no warm congratulations that he was still standing there in front of God.

He might have wanted that, might have expected that, and might have thought that was his due—what he got was a voice from the whirlwind! So when *serious* sufferers stand amazed at God's response, it isn't difficult to understand why. You understand it isn't the pain alone that troubles the heart; it's the apparent senselessness of it all! It's the confusion, the bewilderment, and the seeming chaos of a world that's supposed to be under God's control. And perhaps this is where "Leviathan" and "Behemoth" come in (see 40:15–41:34). The animals in view may be the hippopotamus and the giant crocodile in idealized imagery, bizarre and dangerous, certainly not tamable. They may be standing for, as they often did in ancient and still do in modern times, the impersonal forces and the chaos of chance events.

But even these are part of the will of God (40:15). The wild complexity of nature, the aspects that are beyond human control (like tornadoes, earthquakes and electric storms), are all under the dominion of God. The world is not a tidy place! The world is not all order and predictability. It isn't only ostriches and wild donkeys that laugh at the puny nature of man and put him in his place—you only have to look at hospital wards, diseases and natural disasters to see that Man isn't the god he thinks he is. Whether Job likes it or not, God claims it all as his world and claims control of it all. Whether Job can make sense of it or not, God claims to know what he is doing.

In the face of such overwhelming ignorance, Job should be slow to say he understands all and can make a definitive judgment of all. Maybe he doesn't know everything there is to know about his *own* experience with God. In the face of a God who has been his friend, his generous and intimate friend, Job should have grounds to trust even in his ignorance.

This divine speech mustn't be isolated from the rest of the book because part of its meaning derives from the rest. For the reader there's the prologue and the epilogue; it isn't unbroken mystery and darkness. Nor must the book of Job be isolated from the rest of the Bible! I understand we need to maintain the integrity of the book of Job and look to uncover its specific message. What I don't understand is people taking the book of Job and making it the sole interpreter of our lives today. We can't pretend Jesus hasn't come! We can't pretend we don't know what Job was ignorant of. It's right to look for the darkness in the message of Job but it's surely wrong to say it's all the light we now have! There is enough timeless and profound truth in the book of Job for us to reflect on for a lifetime *but there is Jesus Christ!*

Whatever else we do with the speeches of God, the divine speaker is not simply irresistible power, he isn't a tyrannical sovereign who cares nothing for his creation and this speech is most certainly *not* a study in callousness. Nor is this divine speech a claim by God that he has the right to be unjust. If he wants us to praise him for his righteousness then his righteousness (and goodness) must in some way be recognizable as righteousness. John Stuart Mill is surely right when he says to call God "good" we must have in mind some quality that answers to what we normally call good. If God credits us with the capacity to praise him for his righteousness he must as a consequence be saying something about unrighteousness. As sovereign Lord, God can govern the world any way he sees fit within the moral parameters of his own moral self-revelation.

*Whatever else we do with the speeches of God,
the divine speaker is not simply irresistible power,
he isn't a tyrannical sovereign who cares nothing for
his creation and this speech is most certainly not a
study in callousness. Nor is this divine speech a claim
by God that he has the right to be unjust. . . .
As sovereign Lord, God can govern the world
any way he sees fit within the moral parameters
of his own moral self-revelation.*

24

OSTRICHES AND ASH HEAPS

"But God chose the foolish things of the world to shame the wise;
God chose the weak things of the world to shame the strong."
I Corinthians 1:27

The cataract of questions God pours out on Job serves a number of purposes. This was the man who called on the creation to make his case against God in 12:6-25. Accusing God of giving the robbers peace and the idolaters security (12:6) he then says to his friends, "But ask the animals, and they will teach you, or the birds of the air, and they will tell you; or speak to the earth, and it will teach you, or let the fish of the sea inform you. Which of all these does not know that the hand of the LORD has done this?" (12:7-9).

How wise this Job is. He's so in tune with the creation. Animals, plants, fish and birds all agree with him and anyone who has the sense to understand their teaching as he does will see he is right. Easy enough to say, but when God puts question after question and Job keeps on admitting, 'I don't know, I don't know,' we get a different picture. The poor man isn't as wise as he thought he was. Still, that isn't to say he was a fool because he had known God and followed the creation wisdom down the years. But for all his wisdom, he was abysmally unhappy.

Job, and others like him, really looked the part. They were well versed in the traditions, immaculately correct, perfectly balanced, skilled in their methods and proper in their demeanor. What a contrast to the mother ostrich! Listen to how God describes her in 39:13-18 (NRSV). "The ostrich's wings flap wildly, though its pinions lack plumage. For it leaves its eggs to the earth, and lets them be warmed on the ground, forgetting that a foot may crush them, and that a wild animal may trample them. It deals cruelly with its young, as if they were not its own; though its labor should be in vain, yet it has no fear; because God has made it forget wisdom, and given it no share in understanding. When it spreads its plumes aloft, it laughs at the horse and its rider."

Picture the comical, gawky ostrich watching a group of wise and dignified humans who are going about their business. The contrast can hardly be starker. But how does she survive and prosper when God made her so dim-witted? She obviously knows little about survival since, as the writer describes her (in a section that bristles with linguistic problems) she doesn't know how to treat her eggs or her children? She survives and prospers because there is *grace* in the creation. This gormless creature hasn't the sense to take care of her descendants, so who takes care of all the ostriches? God does. Without a word of thanks from the bird, God protects both her and her eggs sufficiently well that from generation to generation she thrives.

Habel tells us that the words used about her wings and plumage speak of rejoicing and graciousness. In 39:18 for all her silly looks, she laughs at the hunters on horseback. The humans (with all their wisdom) scheme and toil to catch her, but though her wings are flightless, she laughs her head off at her pursuers as she leaves them far behind. So who's the fool? The gawky, comical and dim-witted bird that depends on God or the wise human on his grand steed? She is utterly dependent on God and pays little attention to her offspring. She isn't all tensed up, she doesn't earn her right to live and prosper in the world, she rejoices, laughs and bears grace around with her as she makes her way through the wild creation.

There's something here for Job to learn. Maybe he didn't know as much as he thought, maybe he should have seen God's gracious hand in the world, maybe he should have realized more completely his utter dependence on God. Maybe he didn't need to be so intense, pursuing wisdom to ensure his prosperity through life and maybe he hadn't seen the generosity of God as it could be seen in this gawky, odd, bizarre but wonderfully protected bird.

In 30:29 (RSV and others) he complains that God has isolated and disfigured him. He skulks in the dark like a jackal and with his bizarre appearance he is "a companion of ostriches." Maybe, in light of 39:13-18 that isn't such a bad thing. Maybe ostriches are the right companions for Job right now. Maybe they can teach him something about dependence and grace. Maybe we could all spend a profitable time reflecting on this strange old bird.

We have to ensure our children turn out right and don't make wrong decisions. *We* have to make the right financial moves in a complex world of finance. *We* have to be smart enough, strong enough, swift enough, wise enough, charismatic enough or financially stable enough; after all, we have to run the world.

I'm not sure how to balance all this but at some point we must look in the mirror and simply admit we aren't gods, we aren't wise enough, we're just tiny little people who shouldn't take ourselves too seriously. We need to turn off the lights and tell God we're going to sleep and leave it to him to run the world. Wilbur Rees said it better:

> It's your turn to watch the world, Lord. I have kept it spinning long enough. I have fretted about Wall Street and stewed about the price of eggs. I invested in defense bonds and took out an insurance policy. I wrote my congressman about foreign policy and purchased seat belts for the car. I had the house inspected for termites and had a flu shot. I have worried through the pages of the newspaper at breakfast and the papers of the medical. You'll have to watch the world for a while. I'll leave the light on for you.[13]

It might well be that God was telling Job, "Consider the ostrich of the wilderness, she reasons not, neither does she look classy but verily I say unto you, the sages in all their wisdom and fine dress survive no better than she. If I keep a wise and loving eye on this gawky creature and provide for her what she needs, can I not be trusted to do the same for you?"

Here endeth the lesson.

It might well be that God was telling Job,
"Consider the ostrich of the wilderness,
she reasons not, neither does she look classy
but verily I say unto you, the sages in all their
wisdom and fine dress survive no better than she.
If I keep a wise and loving eye on this gawky
creature and provide for her what she needs,
can I not be trusted to do the same for you?"

25
ABOUT DUST AND ASHES

"Sovereign Lord you trusted me more than I ever wanted you
to trust me and under the burden of that trust I lost my way.
Thank you that by your strong grace the losing of my way
became my path to deeper intimacy with you."

James Keenan

There are only a couple of scholars who think that Job didn't
change as a result of God's appearance and speech to him. As for
the rest, while they disagree over the precise nature of the change,
they insist that Job changed his mind and attitude about *something*.
As Tsevat has said, "The ashes are the same, but it is a changed
man who is sitting in them." Having admitted that God's purposes are unstoppable and that he had been talking out of his league
he claims he has a deeper understanding of God (42:1-5). In light
of all this we have 42:6 which is translated in many ways because
they're all linguistically possible.

"Therefore I despise myself, and repent in dust and ashes"
(NRSV, NIV).
"Therefore I retract, and I repent in dust and ashes" (NASB).
"So I am ashamed of all I have said and repent in dust and
ashes" (TEV).
"I retract all I have said, and in dust and ashes I repent" (JB).
"Therefore I yield, repenting in dust and ashes" (REB).
"And because of that I no longer care about my sufferings;
I have found comfort in spite of this pile of dust and
ashes" (John Gibson in *SJT*, vol. 42.3).
"Therefore, I recant and relent, being but dust and ashes"
(JPS).
"Therefore I retract and repent of dust and ashes" (Habel).

The bulk of scholars agrees that the meaning of this verse can't
be settled by grammar. The Hebrew has no object after the first
verb rendered "despise" or "retract" or "reject" or "recant," or
whatever. So the reader is left to figure out what it is that Job

despises, retracts or rejects. As you can see from the versions, the translators did their own interpreting.

And the second verb, does it mean "repent" or "find comfort" or "relent" concerning dust and ashes? There are good reasons a scholarly consensus tells us it probably isn't "in" dust and ashes but must be "of" or "about" dust and ashes. Repenting 'in' dust and ashes is plain enough since people often expressed their remorse or shame by literally covering themselves with dust and ashes. But what would repent "of" or "concerning" dust and ashes mean? It might mean he changed his view of or about his place on the ash heap.

I think the TEV catches Job's spirit in the first part of the verse. While he did no wrong that triggered the ordeal, he now realizes he has been guilty of colossal pride and scurrilous speech. He's ashamed of himself for that. This changed view of himself, which comes as a result of his deepened understanding of God, means his view of the ash heap, while it remains the same, is also changed.

Dust and ashes he would have rubbed over himself but it seems he made regular pilgrimages to the ash heap (see 2:8). It was to the ash heap the broken-hearted man had taken himself at first as an expression of his grief, but it appears the ash heap had become something else. It seems to have become the visible token of God's heartlessness, of God's faithlessness and injustice. The disfigured little man saw his pile of dust and ashes as a castle built against heaven. It was more than a place of grief, it was a place of protest; more than the location of heartache, it was a center of brave rebellion and a home of gallant resistance. A whole city full of people with a dozen wild horses couldn't have dragged him from there. As long as heaven was the home of injustice, the dust and ashes would be the home of agonized and vocal innocence. That's how he saw it before God talked to him.

Now, a wiser, humbled and submissive Job sees that he must get on with life and leave the ash heap. He confesses no initial wrong, but he no longer accuses God of wrongdoing. His protest is done so he lays down his arms and turns his back on dust and ashes. They no longer serve his purposes; they no longer express his convictions. Since that is true and since he has always been a man of integrity, he can no longer allow the ash heap to be his grimy place of witness against God.

I'm supposing there are some of us who have suffered much and that that suffering became not just the source of heartache but a trigger for resistance. Like a striking employee who walks up and down outside a restaurant with his placard:

**DON'T EAT HERE
MANAGEMENT'S UNFAIR!**

Job, by sitting on his mound of trash, scraping maggots from his ulcers with a piece of pottery proclaims:

**WON'T SERVE HERE
GOD IS UNJUST!**

I'm wondering what it will take to persuade some of us to see that we've got it all wrong, that we've missed the heart of God. I'm wondering what it will take to get us to drop our placards and get on with life. There's nothing dishonorable about doing that, there's no loss of integrity. At one extreme there's the groveling sycophant who thinks God demands the hand-wringing, the overly-humble Uriah Heep stuff. At the other extreme is the liberated modern man who worships what he calls "honesty" and who thinks the *only* proper and genuine response to awful suffering is to verbally abuse God. God deliver us from both!

Somewhere in the middle of all our "honesty" and integrity we're going to have to make room for the God and Father of our Lord Jesus Christ who sent his Son to rescue us (at least Christians should). And if God can put Jesus to grief in order to express his unceasing love for us maybe he can use us in a similar way to bless other people. Maybe our prayers (even those unuttered or defiantly uttered) will be answered and one of these days we'll come to God and tell him, "I'm finished with my strident and unbridled protesting. I see you better now and I repent of dust and ashes."

*Somewhere in the middle of all our "honesty"
and integrity we're going to have to make room
for the God and Father of our Lord Jesus Christ
who sent his Son to rescue us (at least Christians
should). And if God can put Jesus to grief in order to
express his unceasing love for us maybe he can use
us in a similar way to bless other people.
Maybe our prayers (even those unuttered or
defiantly uttered) will be answered and one of
these days we'll come to God and tell him,
"I'm finished with my strident and unbridled
protesting. I see you better now and
I repent of dust and ashes."*

26
ALL'S WELL THAT ENDS WELL

"I had far rather walk, as I do, in daily terror of eternity,
than feel that this was only a children's game in which all the
contestants would get equally worthless prizes in the end."
T.S. Eliot

How's this for a conclusion? "After Job had prayed for his friends, the LORD made him prosperous again and gave him twice as much as he had before. . . . The LORD blessed the latter part of Job's life more than the first. . . . And so he died, old and full of years" (42:10,12,17).

I know in these modern days we aren't supposed to talk about happy endings, but that only makes sense if you have no conviction that all *is* going to end well (even if not pleasantly for some). If you believe as millions of us in every generation have believed—with perfectly good reasons for doing so—the happy endings we see here and now are the promise and prophecy of the ultimate happy ending.

We're supposed to be "realistic" and face life as it is. I'm certain that's true. In fact, Christians can be irritatingly realistic when they keep pointing out that all the talks of reform and of unlimited future improvement through science, medicine, psychology and social theorizings crack up on the rocks of human sinfulness and selfishness. In their more realistic moments these types of Christians will hold us accountable for manufacturing the bulk of all our human ills and will unceasingly call us to be reconciled to God.

Besides, the talkers, movie-makers, philosophizers and liberal activists don't need to lecture the masses about realism because they see more realism in a week than most of these others see in half a lifetime. Of course there's suffering in life and believers have their share of it. They know all about leukemic children, broken marriages, liver cancers, business failures, the trauma of rape and murder. Of course there's grime in human life but do we have to wallow in it? Glory in it? Tirelessly parade it, in order to say that we face it? Go to any street in any city and ask the people there about life "as it really is" and you'll know in a moment that they don't need movies, television or literature to teach them what real life is like.

They need solid reasons for holding to a higher vision which can transform even the present and fill them with hope and joy in the midst of squalor that, at least for a while, can't be changed. Being realistic means we have to take *all* our experience into account. There really *are* happy endings in this life! If we don't know of any happy endings our education is completely lopsided. Life is filled with them.

Successful surgeries, the right medicine found, long lost family members reunited, a threatened marriage redeemed, a lost child found, a war averted, a drug addiction overcome. There are such things as open sewers but there's also the Shimna river that runs from the Mourne Mountains into the Irish sea—clean and pure and tasty. There are pedophiles but there are millions of adults who love, cherish and protect children. There's a Nero but there's an Apostle John, there's a Judas but there's a Jesus Christ, there are adulterous spouses but there are multiplied millions down through the years who not only didn't betray their husbands/wives, they wouldn't dream of it.

One of the crippled aspects of an evil mind is that it thinks because it is diseased every other mind is diseased. Everywhere you look there are happy endings and joyous goings-on. *Of course that's not the whole picture!* But neither is the gloomy one. And there's reason to believe that this "there-must-be-a-dismal-ending" attitude is becoming a bore even to the Hollywood set. A British movie critic asked Tom Cruise, still a prominent movie star, what he had to say in response to those who criticized a movie of his because it was too feel-good and romanticized. Cruise, who's been involved in a lot of "realistic" movies, looked at him for a moment and said, "There's too much cynicism." Another big star, Mel Gibson, in another British talk show, was asked something similar about a movie of his and he responded in precisely the same manner. "They're too cynical," he said. And this is the man who's been in movies as violent as the *Lethal Weapon* series.

Even some biblical scholars are upset because the book of Job ended so well, but there's nothing in the book that requires a sour ending! Job holds his ground, he wasn't accused by God of having violated their relationship, he wasn't required to, nor did he, confess that his wickedness had triggered the ordeal. God remained sovereign with the right to govern the world according to his purposes without having to ask Man's permission and without having to detail his workings to his creatures. It's still the honorable Job we see and it's still the same sovereign Lord; Satan has been answered, humans can and do love God for reasons that transcend the blessing which comes from a relationship with God. So why not a happy ending?

Job is not only at one with God, he is at one with his friends and material/social prosperity returns to him. Yes, but what about the children that died and the mother who suffered the loss of them? How can that be a happy ending? Well, the critics can't have it both ways—either there is a happy ending or there isn't. So the book *is* realistic, it leaves tensions unresolved after all. If that's the case, why would we complain about the over-smoothness of the ending?

But what of the children? We don't need God to detail his response to us to know that "all wrongs will be righted." The Judge of all the earth will do right, said Abraham, and the children of Job are in good hands. And so are all the defenseless, voiceless and forgotten people. If there is a wrong that needs to be righted, the book of Job says we can depend on the gracious but sovereign Lord to work it out. And there is a prophet who speaks in God's name and says to beaten, repentant Israel, "I will restore unto you the years that the caterpillars have eaten."

One more thing before I close this. It seems to me that it's the radically painful or the sometimes sickeningly boring nature of the present reality that assures us of an end that's worth all the trouble. For God to put Job and his loved ones through all that only to bring them to a pathetic finish makes no sense to many of us. Paul was certain that the present suffering is not worthy to be compared with the glory that is to be revealed. There is something of that in what T.S. Eliot said,

> I had far rather walk, as I do, in daily terror of eternity, than feel that this was only a children's game in which all the contestants would get equally worthless prizes in the end.

All's well that ends well!

APPENDIX

MORAL RETRIBUTION

It's clear the ancients, like so many moderns, believed in moral retribution, that is, that God (or the gods) punished evil and rewarded good. The Hebrew/Christian Scriptures take that view and I won't stop to quote texts to prove that. Matatiahu Tsevat thinks that the book of Job goes against all that the Old Testament teaches but be that as it may, the New Testament expressly reaffirms the teaching of the Old Testament. It's true that there is much in the New Testament that speaks of a coming final judgment when matters will be settled but it isn't short of passages that teach God is at work even now showing his wrath against all unrighteousness.

I don't agree with the view that the ancients (in or out of Israel) held to a *rigid* doctrine of moral retribution because that seems to give them too little credit. They would have had to be blind, deaf, and intellectually dumb to believe in anything like a mechanical version of that teaching. Ask yourself, looking at the world you live in, does it *look like* God has retribution built into the fabric of things? Can you see righteous people suffering and wicked people prospering? Of course you can! Do we think these ancients were idiots? The very existence of so many "lament" and "protest" texts in biblical and extra-biblical literature is proof that they thought the world was out of whack. Their eyes and ears told them that reality wasn't structured like a moral vending machine.

Here's how a present scholarly story goes. Israel is in exile, shattered and bewildered. "How did we end up in this mess if we really are the People of God?" they ask. Some believers get together and write Deuteronomy/2 Kings in order to revitalize the nation. One of their central concerns is to explain that the exile was punishment for their wickedness and to affirm the doctrine, "Be good and you'll be blessed, be bad and you'll be cursed." The book of Deuteronomy has the core materials and Joshua through 2 Kings is said to show them operating. The doctrine could hardly be summarized better than in Deuteronomy 30:15-18 where

"Moses" [*Deteronomist*] sets before Israel life and death, prosperity and destruction. Life and prosperity if they obey, death and destruction if they disobey.

But we're told this was a flawed interpretation despite the fact that it gained almost universal acceptance. (We're also told that this doctrine was well established throughout the world before the "Deuteronomist" did his work. I take it that we're supposed to believe Israel had no view of moral government of the world before the exile. That would be strange.)

So there you have it. The central and guiding assumption in all this is that some teachers in exile wrote Deuteronomy/2 Kings to explain why Israel ended up in captivity and they said it was punishment for apostasy. Scholars then tell us these teachers got it wrong anyway. So many psalmists, the writer of Ecclesiastes, some prophetic voices and, notably, the writer of the book of Job all in their own way joined the protest against the flawed interpretation. As one writer put it, "The book of Job is a sustained polemic against the rather simple reward-and-punishment ideology of the popular religion of the day."

Scholars like Tsevat and Crenshaw assure us that books like Job should cure us of any doctrine of moral retribution. Tsevat concedes that the book of Job sets the whole biblical corpus on its ear—it's Job against the rest of the Bible. Obviously the book of Job didn't cure the New Testament writers or Jesus himself since they all continued to proclaim that God punishes evil and rewards goodness and that sometimes he does it in this life. They said these things despite the fact that they were well acquainted with the issues and with the book of Job. But not one of them believed that God (or the gods) built the world like a moral slot machine. In goes your good deed—out comes blessing. In goes your wickedness— out comes cursing/punishment.

Despite the fact that they use ambiguous language at times, many scholars continue to use terms like "rigid" or "exact" or "mechanical" or "measure for measure" to describe the doctrine of retribution the ancient people held. And this form of the doctrine is supposed to explain much of the frustration of the Joban characters. We're told this is why Job was forced to see God as unjust and why Job's friends were compelled to see the man as hypocritically sinful. All four, we're told, held to this rigid version of the doctrine until Job experienced his awful ordeal when, knowing he was innocent of any wrongdoing that would occasion the punishment he was enduring, he began to doubt this ironclad doctrine. In the end they tell us he threw it off completely. The choice was simple: Reject God or the rigid doctrine! If the doctrine was true, the all-knowing God was unrighteous for punishing a man he knew to be innocent. If God was righteous, the rigid doctrine was untrue and should be dumped. (It appears no one thought of dumping the rigid version and holding to a more flexible one but such was the ignorance of those old-timers.)

With this view the friends were willing to rewrite righteous Job's life's history and make him a grievously sinful hypocrite so they could hold on to their cherished but discredited doctrine. Since we know they were wrong about Job, we're supposed to conclude that their doctrine of retribution was false. (Again, it would appear the only available version of that doctrine was the rigid one, otherwise we might have expected them to adopt a more balanced version of it.)

I think this is a misreading of the book of Job because *nobody in the book of Job held to a rigid, mechanical view of retribution!* The poet has all his characters acknowledging that the innocent often suffer and the wicked are often blessed. How could they deny it? Along with Job they saw the truth of that on every street corner, in the face of every godly widow and in the cries of every hungry baby. And furthermore, the very man they were gouging had been blessed beyond measure for years even though they (later) said he had been a hypocrite for years. If he'd been a hypocrite for years how could he have prospered for years under a rigid and mechanical retribution theory? To disprove the mechanical theory you only have to open your eyes and ears, and yet we're told that's what the author of Job undertook to do? But that would be slaying the dead because nobody did or could believe that!

On the other hand, if we take the view that he meant to expose all versions of moral retribution, moderate or rigid, he went about it in a strange way. He gave us the wrong pointer in the prologue when he said it was going to be a question of integrity, it would revolve around a man who *wasn't* punished, and it would end with God restoring blessings to Job. If the deistical views of the world are true the prologue should have said Job was the "luckiest" man in the world rather than saying he was the most richly blessed by God. Let me state what appear to be some very obvious truths about moral retribution.

As revealed in Scripture God's response to wickedness is not mechanically rigid because he retains full personal freedom to act spontaneously. As in a wise and loving family, punishment for wrongdoing 1) may or may not be carried out, 2) may or may not be severe, and 3) is always assessed within the parameters of the loving commitment to the family. If we asked lovingly wise parents if they (in some form) punished wrongdoing, they would say yes. If we asked them if their response against wrongdoing was mechanical and rigid they would say no. And no one would think this strange! Everyone would say that a creative approach to retribution by wise lovers was the way to go. It's certainly the way God approaches it.

Retribution is only one response of a God who is far from being a punishing machine. Retribution is only one "weapon" in the armory of a God who is lovingly committed to all his creatures, making war on what ruins them—wickedness.

Retribution, with God or lovingly wise humans, does not stand in splendid isolation like a sovereign. *Mere* retributive justice cannot show the full-orbed goodness of God. It cannot show God's mercy, grace or long-suffering. Retributive justice seen *within the Story* can be seen as part of the action of a gracious and holy God.

It's true the Bible teaches that God will express his wrath in an ultimate way against all that unrepentantly oppose him, but it's also true that God's judicial anger is not an end in itself. As Abraham Heschel has taught us the aim of God's anger is to remove the reason for the anger in the first place. We rebel against him, he acts in loving judicial anger toward us to bring us back to him that he might not need to be judicially hostile to us. At this point we are to recognize that his anger is in the service of the blessed and gracious relationship he wants with us.

The doctrine that God punishes wickedness and blesses goodness in this life is pervasive and clear enough in Scripture but it's complex and needs to be carefully stated. But why should that surprise us? Say, "God answers prayer!" and hundreds of prickly and many very difficult questions are immediately generated.

The doctrine of retribution is a doctrine about "punishment" and not just "suffering." As soon as we equate suffering with punishment, needless difficulties arise. To speak of "innocent" suffering introduces a *juridical* element with the idea of punishment and blurs the distinction between two related but quite distinct issues, and this itself generates further difficulties.

Here are some questions that will show the complexity of the retribution matter. I'm not suggesting that God sits with wrinkled brow, wringing his hands and wondering how he's going to deal with these complexities. No, he knows what he will do; *we* are the ones who tread water in areas of permanent ignorance as we try to think his thoughts after him.

How do you punish an embezzling parent without causing innocent children to suffer? How do you destroy a wicked man's business without causing hardship to his righteous employees? How do you bless a righteous man's fields without sending the same rain on his unrighteous neighbors around him? How do you withhold rain from the wicked man's fields without putting his righteous neighbor (and his family) to grief? How do you justify blessing a decadent surgeon with surgical brilliance (and consequent material blessings)? How do you bless the innocent child who needs a brilliant surgeon without blessing the decadent surgeon with brilliance? How do you bring a famine or a flood on a nation without bringing suffering on innocent children? How do you punish national wickedness (say, by causing a stock market crash) without putting millions of innocents to grief? How do you send predatory nations against ungodly Israel without hurting innocent babies and thoroughly faithful people? How could you *instantly* punish evil and bless goodness without destroying character and the possibility of personal, creative and loving commitment? (If you don't like these illustrations, find your own.)

In systematizing our understanding of biblical teaching on retribution and reward there are a number of things we need always to keep in mind in order to frame our doctrine with care.

Punishment and suffering are not synonyms! There can be suffering that isn't punishment. The embezzler is jailed for his crime, his innocent children suffer as a consequence. One is suffering and the other is punishment. It isn't wrong for God to allow or bring suffering on someone innocent (Job and the embezzler's child will illustrate) but it would be wrong for God to *punish* someone he knew to be innocent.

God has a loving commitment even to the unrighteous! The Christ claimed it is a fault in us if we love only those who love us and he calls us instead to be like the Father in heaven who loves both the righteous and the unrighteous (Matthew 5:43-47). Paul passionately proclaimed that the true God is Creator of all humans and while he permitted the nations to choose to live without him he continued to bless them with the creation blessings, filling their hearts with joy (Acts 14:14-17). The Psalms proclaim again and again that God blesses all the peoples of the earth (see 67 and 104 as examples). Look again at Jonah 4:1-3 and savor the message there.

Biblical writers will speak of "innocent suffering" even while they assure us that God blesses the righteous! Peter's first epistle illustrates this well. In 3:10-12 he assured us that God blesses the righteous and opposes the wicked, but remarkably, at the same time, he noted that the righteous endure insult and persecution (3:9,14-18). We find the same thing throughout the Old Testament and the rest of the New Testament.

Biblical writers will speak of the wicked prospering and at the same time they will insist that God favors the righteous! Hannah, in 1 Samuel 1 and 2 was well aware of how Peninnah, her jeering rival, prospered but when she got her baby she proclaimed God's favor toward the righteous over against his opposition to the proud and oppressive. She didn't have a lobotomy when she conceived so she wasn't ignorant of other barren but righteous women. Just the same, she took her own experience as one that characterized God as a lifter-up of the lowly and a vindicator of the oppressed. Her blessed experience didn't obliterate her troubled past nor did it deny the ongoing hurt of other women. But her joyous reversal enabled her to interpret her pain to God's honor and assured her that he hadn't forgotten the other troubled women. Her experience becomes a model.

God's blessings for the righteous must be appropriated by the righteous! The Old Testament characteristically speaks of blessing in terms of material prosperity and lays the credit for blessing at God's feet. But all the sunshine and rain in the world will not produce a crop if the farmer will not plough, sow, and harvest. It's true that even these activities go back to God's grace but the human must cooperate with the God who blesses. (Precisely how to say where and how the divine initiative and human response meet is beyond us.) If the human will not work the land, the blessing is not secured. Following on from this, there are those (family, poor) who depend on these farmers for the blessings from God so the farmers are the channel of God's blessing. If the farmers won't work, not only do they suffer themselves, but also those depending on them suffer, even though it is God's intention for them all to be blessed.

Because God is lovingly committed to all his creatures, he experiences a "conflict of interests." I don't mean by this that he is forced to dither in a state of indecision.

God loves the oppressor, Nineveh, as the book of Jonah proclaims, so he tolerates, calls to repentance, and blesses any move in his direction. But God also loves the peoples oppressed by Nineveh, so we have the book of Nahum that speaks of Nineveh's awful exclusion. God's act against Nineveh was no loveless retribution, it was a necessary tragedy; it was God acting in love on behalf of the smaller nations (many of whom were not righteous!).

These truths would be part of the explanation for God's refusal to exercise instant and mechanical judgment against wickedness. In the terms of 2 Peter 3:9 the delay in judging is loving reluctance in favor of the wicked but the certainty of judgment in favor of the innocent and oppressed.

The Scriptures teach that there is a hierarchy of blessings and that some may be withheld so others might be fully enjoyed. Jeremiah lives without the blessings of family that he might be God's voice to the nation. Righteous Jews suffer exile with the guilty that they might be the channel of blessing to the world. Many despise a second or third car or extra income to gain more time with children and family. Joseph loses years of parental affection to become a savior of his own and other people. Moses says no to vast wealth to gain a greater reward.

Who among us, daily, *doesn't* reject genuine but minor joys in order to gain the greater blessings? Is depth of character more to be prized than possessing a TV set or a Rolls Royce car? Who doesn't know the parables of the hidden treasure and the pearl of great price (Matthew 13)? And who doesn't agree with the spirit and thrust of them? Does God cheat us when on occasions he withholds the good that he might give us the better or the best?

The Scriptures teach that what appears to be a blessing may be a curse and what appears to be a curse may be a blessing. When God punished Israel at the hands of the Assyrian, he gave Assyria success but success wasn't a blessing (see Isaiah 10:5-7). When God had Joseph dragged off to slavery in Egypt he subjected him to curse though in fact, it was all blessing (see Genesis 39–41 and 50:20). When Job was slandered by Satan, God went to his defense by putting him to grief.

The Scriptures teach that God may put the innocent to grief in order to bless others, even the unrighteous. The Joseph story illustrates this well. Not only are the nations all around Egypt blessed through the captivity and pain of this young man, the house of Potiphar is blessed through his presence (Genesis 39:2-5). In our world we prize vicarious suffering, we admire those who choose loss that others might be benefited, we call them heroes. And it isn't a rare thing (scan the Scriptures) for God to keep creation blessings from his willing servants that others might be blessed. Shouldn't we admire him for it? See this shown and stated at its grandest in passages like Isaiah 53 and 1 Peter 2:21-24.

Punishment is more than giving an individual what he "deserves." It's true that retribution points to the transgressor and the fact that he has done wrong, but it also speaks volumes about the values of a society. Putting the best face on it, punishment proclaims to everyone what is acceptable and unacceptable on a moral/social level. Punishment is not supposed to be an act of spleen-easing revenge by a society (or a god) on a rebel; it speaks to the society itself and offers homage to a righteousness that has been spurned. Punishment is righteousness made present *as* suffering and it is supposed to honor, educate and shape people in righteousness.

Since mere *retribution cannot exhibit grace, compassion, nor forgiveness it cannot create or nurture the full character or heart of God or nourish loving devotion.* If God handed out instant and complete punishment for every sinful thought, word, deed, attitude, mixed motive and omission (in short, for everything that is unlike the Christ) what kind of life would we live? Imagine God giving us an electric shock for every manifestation of unChristlikeness. Imagine an electric shock not only for wrongs done but good left undone. We'd never stop jerking and jumping.

If God instantly and fully rewarded goodness would this generate love for him and others or a preoccupation with *reward* and *punishment?* Could a healthy/loving human relationship exist and flourish under these circumstances? Imagine God giving us an electric shock immediately and every time we thought, spoke or acted unlike Christ. Think this through for a moment and try to say what kind of world it would be, what kind of persons we would be.

Bearing in mind the character of God and the kind of people he purposes to nurture . . . instant, mechanical, and rigid retribution is *not* an option for him. However, some form of retribution is defensible on the grounds that it *can* be used to nurture, promote goodness, and mark evil as unacceptable without overwhelming humans by either reward or punishment.

ABOUT THE AUTHOR

Jim McGuiggan is a native of Belfast, Northern Ireland. After several years of teaching and preaching in America, he has returned to Ireland where he lives with his wife, Ethel, and ministers with a congregation outside Belfast. He is the author of numerous books including *The God of the Towel*; *Jesus, Hero of Thy Soul*; *Where the Spirit of the Lord Is . . .*; *Celebrating the Wrath of God*, and *The Dragon Slayer: the Saving of a World*.

NOTES

Chapter 1
[1] The Turgenev incident is re-told in James Burns, *Illustrations for Preachers and Teachers* (London: James Clarke, n.d.), pp. 202-203.

Chapter 2
[2] Thomas Hauser, *Muhammed Ali* (New York: Simon & Schuster, 1991), p. 480.

[3] Ibid., 382.

Chapter 3
[4] "The Idylls of the King," from *The Works of Alfred Lord Tennyson* (Hertfordshire, England: Wordsworth Poetry Library, 1994), p. 526.

[5] F.W Robertson, *Sermons*, 4th Series (London: Kegan, Paul, Trench, 1891), p. 131.

Chapter 4
[6] Paul Scherer, *The Interpreter's Bible*, vol. 3 (Nashville: Abingdon, 1954), p. 929.

Chapter 5
[7] "Isn't This a Lovely Day to Be Caught in the Rain," 1935, words and music by Irving Berlin for the movie *Top Hat*, directed by Mark Sandrich, scripted by Dwight Taylor and Alan Scott from a play by Alexander Farago and Aladar Laszlo.

Chapter 12
[8] J.H. Jowett quoted in R.M. Miller, *Harry Emerson Fosdick* (New York: OUP, 1985), p. 59.

[9] Charles L. Campbell, *Interpretation* (October, 1997), p. 385.

Chapter 16
[10] E.L. Allen, *The Self and Its Hazards* (New York: The Philosophical Library, 1951), pp. 39-40 quoted in Paul Scherer, *The Interpreter's Bible*, vol. 3, p. 986.

Chapter 22
[11] Reinhold Niebuhr, *Beyond Tragedy: Essays on the Christian Interpretation of History* (Freeport, NY: Books for Libraries Press, 1971), p. 97.

Chapter 23
[12] Elie Weisel, *Night* (London: Penguin Books, 1981), p. 79—surely a "must read" book in which he speaks for all the plundered and oppressed.

Chapter 24
[13] Wilbur Rees, *$3.00 of God* (Valley Forge: Judson Press, 1971), p. 64.

LaVergne, TN USA
01 March 2011
218360LV00009B/30/A